INTERPRETING
DREAMS

INTERPRETING DREAMS

A HISTORY OF DREAM ANALYSIS

RICHARD CRAZE

southwater

This edition is published by Southwater, an imprint of Anness Publishing Ltd, Hermes House, 88–89 Blackfriars Road, London SE1 8HA; tel. 020 7401 2077; fax 020 7633 9499

www.southwaterbooks.com; www.annesspublishing.com

If you like the images in this book and would like to investigate using them for publishing, promotions or advertising, please visit our website www.practicalpictures.com for more information.

UK agent: The Manning Partnership Ltd; tel. 01225 478444; fax 01225 478440; sales@manning-partnership.co.uk
UK distributor: Grantham Book Services Ltd; tel. 01476 541080; fax 01476 541061; orders@gbs.tbs-ltd.co.uk
North American agent/distributor: National Book Network; tel. 301 459 3366; fax 301 429 5746; www.nbnbooks.com
Australian agent/distributor: Pan Macmillan Australia; tel. 1300 135 113; fax 1300 135 103; customer.service@macmillan.com.au
New Zealand agent/distributor: David Bateman Ltd; tel. (09) 415 7664; fax (09) 415 8892

A CIP catalogue record for this book is available from the British Library.

ETHICAL TRADING POLICY

Because of our ongoing ecological investment programme, you, as our customer, can have the pleasure and reassurance of knowing that a tree is being cultivated on your behalf to naturally replace the materials used to make the book you are holding. For further information about this scheme, go to www.annesspublishing.com/trees

Publisher: Joanna Lorenz
Editorial Director: Helen Sudell
Executive Editor: Joanne Rippin
Additional Text: Raje Airey and Jenny Barrett
Picture Research: Frances Vargo
Designer: Adelle Morris
Production Controller: Darren Price

Previously published as part of a larger volume, *Dream Dictionary*

CONTENTS

INTRODUCTION

In practically every age and culture, dreams have fascinated and puzzled us and we have constantly searched for ways to understand their significance and to interpret their meaning. There is a famous story told by the Taoist philosopher Chuang-tzu (399-295 BC). While sleeping he had a dream in which he dreamt he was a butterfly. He could fly and land on flowers, drawing up nectar and feeling the warmth of the sun on his wings. The dream was so vivid that when he woke he couldn't decide who he was: was he a man dreaming he was a butterfly, or could he be a butterfly dreaming he was a man?

When we sleep we drift into another dimension, a dimension that is not bound by space or time. In this magical land the impossible becomes possible, and the nonsensical appears perfectly plausible. This is the land of dreams, a mysterious shape-shifting world where boundaries dissolve and merge, so that when we wake it can take a moment to distinguish between what is a dream and what is not. As Chuang-tzu's story illustrates, our dreams can cause us to question how we see the world and ourselves and how we define what is "real". This is not to say that there is genuine confusion between the outer world in which we live our lives and the world of dreams. Where confusion exists, it is usually labelled insanity. Rather it is an acknowledgement of a different dimension and of a different experience. For dreams are from the inner world, having their own internal logic and subjective meaning, and are as valid in their own way as what is happening in the world "out there".

VALUING DREAMS

Among many cultures the dream experience is valued and the mysteries of sleep and dreaming are taken seriously. Whenever this is the case, dream interpretation is also valued. In early cultures for instance, shamans, priests or sages were consulted and their position in society was revered. For a long time in Western society, an interest in dreams went underground. Dreams were variously associated with insanity or were the work of the devil, or were simply written off as meaningless nonsense. These attitudes were revolutionized in the 20th century with fresh insights from science and psychotherapy. Since then our interest in dreams has been growing at a remarkable rate, as more and more of us search for ways to make sense of our lives and to fulfil our potential. We are recognizing that our dreams, far from being nonsense or a sign of mental illness, often contain intriguing and valuable information, which, once decoded, can help us understand our subconscious. We are also learning how to become our own dream interpreters.

ABOUT THIS BOOK

This book is a guide to making sense of dreams. It recognizes that no two people are exactly alike and therefore no two dreams are the same. When interpreting dreams the book takes the view that it is experience rather than theory that counts: you can become your own dream expert. This approach is very different to many dream dictionaries where it is possible to "look up" the meaning of a particular dream symbol or theme and "apply" it to your dream. For instance, you may dream of a tree. Some dream books may say that a tree signifies growth, and if it is bearing fruit, that it prophesies abundance and wealth. What they fail to do is encourage you to look at the tree itself and find out what it means for you. To do this is to approach your dream and yourself with a spirit of enquiry, asking questions about the dream content in order to arrive at your own understanding.

The book contains chapters on the history, nature and sense of dreams and is intended to give an overview of dream theories, past and present. The information that this provides can help you recognize different types of dream and dream symbols, including those that Jung described as coming from the collective unconscious, embodied in the archetypes we all recognize. The final chapter, Working with Dreams, offers practical suggestions for how to work with your own dreams. Keeping a dream diary, working with dream tools and using your dreams for problem-solving as well as learning how to control them are some of the ways you can work with your dreams. With keys such as dream tools, dream catchers, dream guides, and various techniques for analysing your personal dream world, you will be able to unlock the secrets of your dreams. This will bring a greater understanding of yourself and your relationships, and increase your capacity to live life to the full.

It is hoped that you will find what is here both illuminating and stimulating and can use it as a springboard for further discovery. Remember, dreams come from the dark, the time of the moon, madness and mystery. To understand them, you need to feel your way around, using intuition and instinct rather than reason and logic, and so begin to unlock the secrets of the night.

Trust in dreams, for in them is the hidden gate to eternity.   KAHLIL GIBRAN

ABOVE Artists for centuries have tried to portray their dreams in pictorial representation. What they paint and what we dream may not seem the same but we share the same need to purge the internal demons of dream.

LEFT Images of dreams are but an instant, frozen in time forever, whereas in reality our dreams are flexible, ongoing, and changing rapidly and continuously.

BELOW Surrealist art for most people seems to come closest to how we sense our dreams and may help us to convey the feel of a dream, if not its reality.

ABOVE Sometimes an artist does seem to crystallize a moment in a dream that can haunt us all of our lives.

WHY WE DREAM

THERE ARE FEW THINGS WE DO WITH SUCH REGULARITY AND INTENSITY AS SLEEP AND DREAM. WE SPEND ALMOST ONE THIRD OF OUR LIVES SLEEPING AND WE DREAM — ON AVERAGE FOR A TOTAL OF TWO HOURS OR SO — EVERY NIGHT. YET PRECISELY WHY WE DREAM IS STILL UNCERTAIN. MANY THEORIES HAVE BEEN PUT FORWARD: FOR THE SCIENTIST, DREAMS ARE A PRODUCT OF A CERTAIN KIND OF SLEEP AND A WAY FOR THE BRAIN TO PROCESS IMPORTANT DATA; FOR THE MYSTIC, THEY ARE AN OPPORTUNITY FOR THE SOUL TO LEAVE THE BODY AND EXPERIENCE OTHER DIMENSIONS; WHILE FOR THE PSYCHOLOGIST THEY REPRESENT THE WORKINGS OF THE UNCONSCIOUS MIND.

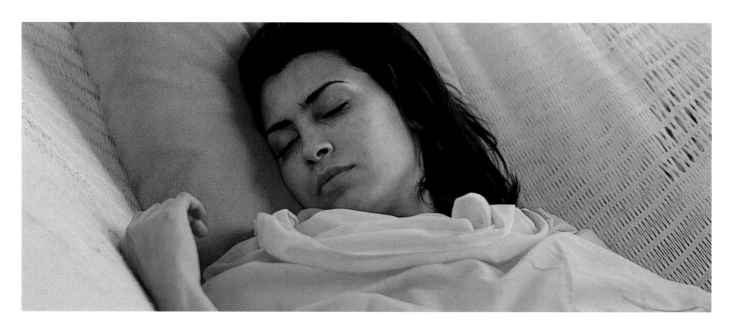

ABOVE Whatever we think we know about dreams is forgotten when we fall asleep and enter the strange reality of the dream world, where physical laws are suspended and a different reality takes place.

SLEEP PATTERNS

Through a night of around seven to eight hours of undisturbed sleep, we experience two alternating types of sleep: orthodox or slow-wave deep sleep, and paradoxical or light sleep. Orthodox sleep lasts for about 90 minutes, and is followed by a shorter period of paradoxical sleep. Paradoxical sleep is marked by rapid eye movements (REM) and it is during this type of sleep that we dream. This alternating cycle goes on through the night, with the REM phase gradually increasing in length with each subsequent cycle, until after about seven or eight hours' sleep it can last for up to half an hour or more. As we get older, the length of time we spend in REM sleep diminishes, while at the other end of the scale, it has been found that young babies spend extended periods of time in REM.

THE ROLE OF DREAMING

Scientific research also indicates that in the later stages of gestation the unborn child exhibits signs of REM activity in the womb. This has led to the

suggestion that dreaming is somehow linked with human growth and development. Similarly, laboratory testing has shown that if you deprive people of REM sleep, the subject becomes unwell very fast. Within a few days, unpleasant symptoms such as depression, anxiety, nausea, irritability and general disorientation are experienced. Irrespective of whether or not we remember them, it seems our dreams play an important part in health and wellbeing. It has even been suggested that we sleep in order to dream.

A LITTLE DEATH

Many believe that our dreams are also linked with spiritual growth. In some esoteric traditions for instance, sleep is regarded as an intermediate stage between life and death. Every night we experience a "little death" as we fall into unconsciousness, and dreams are regarded as gateways into altered states of mind. Learning how to navigate the world of dreams becomes an important preparation for when the soul will eventually leave the body permanently

at death. Initiates are taught how to prepare themselves for sleep and dreaming, learning how to influence the dreaming state and to bring back experiences from the dream world.

THE POWER OF THE UNCONSCIOUS

This dream world is not something that exists outside of ourselves but resides deep within. In psychological terms, it is regarded as a product of the unconscious mind.

The unconscious may be described as the deepest level of the psyche in which impulses are held in a dynamic, but repressed state. In contrast to the relatively small proportion of things of which we are aware, the unconscious is a massive storehouse of memories, dreams and reflections, both personal and, some believe, transpersonal. By bringing unconscious material up from the hidden depths of the mind and out into the open, our dreams are a way of gaining greater self-knowledge. They are a way of increasing our conscious awareness and becoming wise. From this perspective, dreams are no longer seen as messages from gods or other independent agents outside of ourselves, but as messages from within.

LEFT Sometimes we don't remember our dreams but that doesn't mean they aren't continually occurring in our sleeping minds.
BELOW Do babies still in the womb dream? And if they do, where on earth do their dream images and impulses come from?

THE LANGUAGE OF DREAMS

In order to interpret these messages from the unconscious, we need to understand the language of dreams. During the day, the conscious mind is in control and we negotiate the everyday world through reason and logic. At night, the unconscious mind takes over and enters the dream world, using visual imagery, symbols and metaphors. These can elicit a deep emotional response. To understand our dreams we need to listen with the heart rather than the head, developing our intuition while temporarily suspending judgement and disbelief.

We are such stuff
As dreams are made on;
and our little life
Is rounded with a sleep.

WILLIAM SHAKESPEARE, THE TEMPEST

ANIMALS' SLEEP

Dreaming does not seem to be confined to human beings. Different animal species also exhibit signs of REM sleep and dreaming. Cats, for instance, enter deep-wave sleep about 30 minutes after sleep onset. In that condition, their neck muscles are fully relaxed and slight twitching of the rest of the body may be observed. Although we do not know what the cat is experiencing, we assume that it is a vivid dream.

DREAMING THROUGH HISTORY

Since time immemorial, our dreams have been a source of awe and wonder. At various points in history, they have been seen as messages from the gods, and supernatural experiences involving visions of the future, as well as indications of the state of our physical and mental health. Dreams have been used to shed light on the past, gain understanding of the present, and even to predict the future. This has not only been true for individuals, but also for whole nations. Some dreams have even changed the course of history.

In this section we will look at how dreams have been regarded through the ages, in the ancient and classical world, in India and the Far East, in Europe and in traditional societies. We will also look at the important role they have played in some of the world's major religions, including Buddhism, Christianity and Islam.

SINCE THE DAWN OF TIME

How long is it since we began dreaming? We have no sure way of knowing, but stretching back into the mists of prehistory, cave paintings in France from the Neanderthal period seem to indicate some sort of dream drawings above the heads of the hunters. Thousands of years later when people began to discover ways of writing, they noted down their dreams. We know that dreaming was an important part of life in the ancient civilizations of Sumer, Assyria, Babylonia and Egypt. Dreams were associated with divine or supernatural powers, and temples were dedicated to the gods of dreams.

THE FIRST DREAM RECORDS

Clay tablets dating back to around 3000 BC provide some of the earliest surviving writings of the human race. These tablets include the dream books of the Assyrians and Babylonians, discovered at Ninevah in the library of Ashurbanipal (c.669-626 BC), an Assyrian king. Other similar tablets were discovered during excavations of a pyramid-type temple at E-zida, in Mesopotamia, on the top of which was a shrine to Nabu, the Sumerian god of wisdom. The tablets' cuneiform script reveals fragments of the Babylonian epic of Gilgamesh, the legendary warrior king of Sumer. They also tell us about Gilgamesh's dreams and how his mother, the goddess Ninsun, interprets them. Her interpretation is often credited with being the first dream analysis, or at least the first for which we have a written record.

THE DREAMS OF GILGAMESH

Night after night, the aggressively powerful warrior king of Sumer, Gilgamesh, was troubled by bad dreams. Disturbed, Gilgamesh takes the dreams to his mother, who tells him that someone as powerful as himself is about to enter his life. She predicted that his struggles to gain supremacy over the newcomer will fail, but that the two men will become close companions and together achieve great feats. Later on in the epic, Ninsun's interpretation proves correct when Gilgamesh meets Enkidu, a "wild man" (an embodiment of an uncivilized, "primordial" human) who does indeed become his friend and helps bring Gilgamesh back down to earth. Further on in the tale, Gilgamesh is warned in another dream of the death of Enkidu, which also comes to pass.

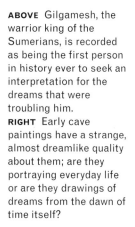

ABOVE Gilgamesh, the warrior king of the Sumerians, is recorded as being the first person in history ever to seek an interpretation for the dreams that were troubling him.
RIGHT Early cave paintings have a strange, almost dreamlike quality about them; are they portraying everyday life or are they drawings of dreams from the dawn of time itself?

PORTENTOUS DREAMS

The primary interest in dreams at this time seems to have been in the salutary warnings they could provide about the future, although dreams were also used as a form of gambling, where the dream symbols were used to predict lucky wins. Furthermore the Assyrian and Babylonian dream books also reveal a concern with the dangerous aspect of dreams, allegedly sent by demons and spirits of the dead. To protect themselves from such harmful influences, people built temples to Mamu, the Babylonian goddess of dreams, and propitiatory rites were practised in her name. An Za Qa, the god of dreams, was recognized and worshipped by the Sumerians, Assyrians and Babylonians.

MYTHOLOGY OF DREAMS

Looking at the mythology of any ancient civilization has been likened to reading a dream. That is because these stories represent what are sometimes referred to as the "cultural pattern dreams" of that civilization. In other words, the gods and goddesses, the heroes and villains, and the shapes and symbols of the stories are the same ones that people would have dreamt of night after night. These characters represent what are known as "archetypal" images, presenting us with the themes and concerns that have always struck a chord deep within the heart and soul of humankind. Irrespective of time or place, these stories are able to teach or remind us of universal truths.

ABOVE In Babylon vast temples were built dedicated to Mamu, the Babylonian goddess of dreams; and dream interpretation was elevated to the status of a religion.

THE GODDESS ISHTAR

Throughout the ancient world, the Moon was worshipped in various forms. The Babylonian goddess Ishtar was known as Ashtarte in Canaan, Isis in ancient Egypt and Artemis in ancient Greece. Like the moon in its waxing aspect, the goddess is a symbol of fertility and all life emanates from her, yet like the waning or dark moon, she is also the destroyer, the one who disappears into the darkness. However, like the crescent moon, the goddess is reborn and appears once again in her beneficent aspect.

The story of Ishtar's descent into the underworld, where she is tortured and bleeds to death before being revived by the twins Plant and Water of Life, is a myth of regeneration, symbolizing the cyclical nature of life and the passage between worlds.

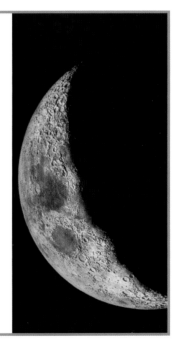

And the goddess Ishtar appeared to each man in a dream, saying: 'I will march before Ashurbanipal, the king whom I have created'.

BABYLONIAN LEGEND

ANCIENT EGYPT

Like the Babylonians, the Egyptians also regarded
dreams as warnings, although they believed they
came from the gods rather than from spirits or
demons. The Egyptians viewed dreams as a portal, a
gateway to another world which they passed
through every night. Here in this other world they
could travel in their astral or "dream body",
gathering knowledge of far distant places,
conversing with the gods and meeting with the
spirits of the dead. In general, dreams were regarded
as helpful, although they could also be malevolent.
In order to avert disaster the gods demanded
penance and sacrifices, although they would also
answer questions put to them by the dreamer in a
practice known as "dream incubation".

DREAM INCUBATION

The practice of dream incubation was widely
observed throughout the ancient world, although
our first record of it comes from ancient Egypt.
Throughout the land, a number of temples, known
as "serapeums", were dedicated to Serapis, the god
of dreams and dreaming. The most famous of these
was at Memphis, dating back to around 3000 BC.

Thebes was another important site. It was in such
temples that dream incubation was practised. This
was an intensely ritualistic procedure intended to
encourage an especially informative dream from the
gods. Dream incubation seems to have been very
popular and was used for a variety of purposes,
including seeking remedies for particular illnesses,
obtaining guidance on relationship and/or personal
issues and predicting what the future had in store.
The practice was often dedicated to Imhotep, the
god of healing.

INCUBATION RITUALS

Ritualistic preparations for dream incubation were
extremely complex and could last for several days.
Typically the incubant (the dreamer) would take part
in purification practices, such as fasting, bathing and
abstaining from sex, they would also make prayers
and offerings to the gods. Sometimes harmless
snakes were placed around the dreamer's bed at the
serapeum and the dreamer would then go to sleep
with his or her request in mind. Through their own
rituals, while the dreamer slept, the temple priests
often helped to "seed" the dreamer's request. At
times a "stand-in" dreamer was used in place of the

THE DREAM OF THOTMES IV

One very early prophetic dream dates back to around 1420 BC. It is recorded on a sheet of granite and held between the paws of the great sphinx at Giza where it can still be seen today (right).

While sleeping next to the sphinx, Thotmes dreamt that he would one day be ruler of Egypt and have a long and prosperous reign. However, for the dream to come true, the gods told Thotmes that he had to clear away the sand from the statue. At that time, the sphinx was neglected and beginning to disappear under the sand.

When Thotmes awoke he did as he had been instructed and then vowed to keep the sphinx clean and well cared for, for the rest of his life. Thotmes later went on to become one of Egypt's pharaohs.

person who was seeking help. The stand-in would be someone who was known to be a gifted dreamer. When the dreamer or the stand-in awoke, the dream would be related to the oracles or priests for their interpretation.

DREAM INTERPRETATIONS

Ancient Egyptian papyri reveal some of the conclusions the Egyptians reached about dream interpretation. One document, dating back to the 13th dynasty (1770 BC), concludes that if a woman dreams of kissing her husband, trouble lies ahead. This is an example of "opposites", in which it is thought that a dream means the reverse of what it appears to suggest.

One of the most famous dream records of the Egyptian era is the "Chester Beatty" papyrus, which was inscribed around 1350 BC. It came from Thebes and contains references to around 200 dreams, many of which date from an earlier period. Particularly interesting are the details of three modes of interpretation, which anticipate principles used by Freud centuries later, these are the detection of hidden associations, the use of opposites, and the use of visual or verbal puns.

DREAM PUNS

Puns in the world of dream interpretation are rather like games of free association, where one thing reminds us of another. Sometimes these "meanings" are catalogued and get handed down in dream dictionaries, where they appear as utter nonsense to later generations, whose cultural references and language are completely different. For instance, the Chester Beatty papyrus reveals that in ancient Egypt to dream about bare buttocks means the dreamer is about to lose his or her parents. This may seem absurd until we realize that the word used for "buttocks" closely resembled the word for "orphan".

DISPOSING OF BAD DREAMS

For dealing with a recurring bad dream, the ancient Egyptians had a curious ritual. On waking after another night of the same dream they would blow out their breath into a special receptacle – usually a wooden cup – which was then thrown into the fire. This symbolic act represented "burning" the dream, its negative power would be destroyed by the fire so that it could never return to haunt the dreamer.

THE CLASSICAL WORLD

ONEIROLOGY IS THE STUDY OF DREAMS. THIS WORD IS DERIVED FROM "ONEIROS", THE WORD FOR DREAMS IN THE ANCIENT GREEK LANGUAGE. LIKE THEIR KNOWLEDGE IN SO MANY AREAS, THE ANCIENT GREEKS' UNDERSTANDING OF DREAMS WAS ESPECIALLY SOPHISTICATED AND SEVERAL WELL-KNOWN THINKERS OF THE DAY DEBATED AND GAVE THEIR INSIGHTS ON THE SUBJECT. THIS INFORMATION WAS LATER EXTENDED AND CLASSIFIED BY THE ROMANS TO GIVE US A WIDE BODY OF KNOWLEDGE FROM THE CLASSICAL WORLD. BOTH CIVILIZATIONS USED DREAMS AS A FORM OF PREDICTION AND AS A WAY OF GAINING INSIGHTS INTO THE MIND OF THE DREAMER.

GATES OF HORN AND IVORY

The earliest mention of dreams in Greek literature is from Homer. We have little information about Homer or his life, but many historians date his era as some time in the 700s BC. We know that at this time there was widespread belief in the divine origin of dreams, which were regarded as messages to humanity from Zeus, communicated by Hypnos, the god of sleep and his son Morpheus, the god of dreams. However, not all dreams were necessarily reliable. Homer distinguishes between true and false dreams, writing that true dreams come through a "gate of horn", and false through an "ivory gate". Such distinctions were not merely of theoretical interest, as to act on a false dream as if it were true could have disastrous consequences. Centuries later for instance the Persian leader Xerxes' dreams falsely convinced him that an attack on Athens would end victoriously. Acting on this advice Xerxes led his army to destruction in 480 BC.

HOMER'S ODYSSEY

In his epic work *The Odyssey*, Homer enlarges on the idea of true and false dreams through the character of Penelope, who remarks that dreams are awkward and confusing, for what is in them does not necessarily come true. She says: "There are two gates through which these insubstantial visions reach us; one is of horn and the other of ivory. Those that come through the ivory gate cheat us with empty promises that never see fulfilment; while those that issue from the gate of burnished horn inform the dreamer what will really happen".

SIGNIFICANT AND NON-SIGNIFICANT DREAMS

Influenced perhaps by Homer's ideas, the ancient Greeks also distinguished between two types of dream: the significant and the non-significant. Significant dreams were the ones which came from the gods. These were the ones that people wanted to have when they were about to undertake an important project, such as a business venture, a voyage or a new relationship. The non-significant dreams were more personal to the dreamer. The gods played no part in these and the way they are reported makes them sound more like the sort of dream we experience, for the most part, today.

DREAMS AND HEALING

The tradition of healing temples and dream incubation is one that was continued by both the Greeks and Romans, especially for acquiring information to treat disease. In ancient Greece famous sleep temples at Oropos and Epidaurus were

BELOW Homer, seen here being honoured by the gods, made the distinction between true and false dreams, and talked of the danger of being unable to distinguish between the two.

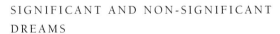

dedicated to Asklepios, the god of medicine, although it is believed that hundreds more temples existed throughout the ancient and classical world. The temples were situated in places of natural beauty, surrounded by fragrant plants and herbs, natural springs or shady forests. Another common feature was the serpent, and today the ruins at Epidaurus show us the pit where snakes were kept for healing and incubation purposes. This association of snakes with healing developed into the familiar symbol of the "caduceus", a healing staff entwined by two serpents. Today this symbol is widely used by many healing professions.

HIPPOCRATES

Known as the father of modern-day medicine, the Greek doctor, Hippocrates (460-377 BC), accepted that some dreams were of divine origin and could prophesy events. He endeavoured to put this capacity to scientific use by using the symbolism of dreams to diagnose the dreamer's state of health, associating the microcosm of the human body with the macrocosm of the universe. In his *Treatise on Dreams*, for instance, Hippocrates asserts that bright

stars in a dream indicate good health, whereas to dream of dim stars precedes illness. Dreaming of flowing rivers, he states, indicates problems with the urinary system, while dreaming of floods points to an excess of blood and the need to "bleed" the patient. Such dreams are referred to by Hippocrates as prodromal, from the Greek word *prodromos*, meaning "running before".

ABOVE Hippocrates, the Greek physician, believed dream interpretation was connected to physical sickness – if you dreamt of a specific sickness or disease it meant that you were suffering from it in real life.

THE DELPHIC ORACLE

The word "oracle" also means "answer" and oracle dreams were incubated at the famous site in Delphi (left), widely believed in ancient times to be the centre of the world. The site was situated on sulphurous hot springs and its entrance bore the inscription "know thyself". Hallucinogenic plants, such as henbane and jimsonweed, were burned to put the seer of the oracle into a trance, and make them ready to receive dreams and visions from the gods.

ABOVE Some Greek philosophers would have nothing to do with dream interpretation, whereas others were convinced that dreams had mystical importance. The two groups debated the issue endlessly.

THE PHILOSOPHERS

It would be wrong to assume that all Greeks subscribed to the mystical significance of dreams. Many famous thinkers challenged this notion and their ideas have been highly influential in the way dreams are regarded by Western society. Heraclitus (450-375 BC) is generally regarded as the first person on record to proffer a purely rational explanation. Far from being a communication from the gods, he asserted, someone's dream world is entirely personal to them. It has nothing to do with anything outside of the dreamer's mind and is simply an ordinary experience, having less significance than anything that happens while in waking consciousness. However, perhaps more than any other thinker, it is Aristotle (384-322 BC) who comes closest to our modern way of looking at the meaning of dreams.

ARISTOTLE'S CONTRIBUTION

From his observations of sleeping animals, Aristotle concludes that it is not only humans who have dreams. He uses this as evidence to counter any theory that dreams have any divine or cosmic pattern or that they have any particular significance. He also notes that since all external sensations are reduced or absent during sleep, subjective sensations must be highlighted. He goes on to assert that dream images can have an influence on subsequent behaviour. In that sense dreams can be prophetic, as our thoughts are influenced by what we have seen during sleep. He also claims that the insights

THE EMPEROR'S DREAMS

After Calpurnia's prophetic dream about her husband, Julius Caesar, Caesar's heir, the emperor Augustus (above) (63 BC-AD 14), made a law declaring that anyone having a dream about the emperor's welfare should announce it in the marketplace. According to another historical text, Tranquillus' *Lives of the Caesars* Augustus set such store by dreams that he made a fool of himself. He went about Rome begging for alms because it had been predicted that he would do so in a dream.

available from dreams are like objects reflected in water: when the water of the mind is calm, the images are easy to see, when the water is troubled, the reflections become distorted. He says that the more the mind can be calmed before sleep, the more the dreamer can learn. Aristotle's theories were outlined in three seminal works: *On Dreams, On Sleep and Waking* and *On Prophecy in Sleep*.

DREAMS AND THE HUMAN PSYCHE

In his theories, Aristotle also links the hallucinations of the mentally ill, the illusions of ordinary people and the content of dreams and fantasies, concluding that they may all share a common origin – an idea which was later developed by the 20th-century psychologist, Carl Jung. Plato (427-347 BC), another of the Greek philosophers, also had ideas about dreams which predate 20th-century psychology. He describes the human psyche as possessing "a lawless, wild beast nature which peers out in sleep". As we

no longer exercise rational control while sleeping, our lust and rage can enjoy free and full expression. Centuries later, such a view would be central to Sigmund Freud's ideas about defining human personality and behaviour.

PROPHETIC DREAMS IN ROME

Accounts of prophetic dreams have occurred throughout history with some of the most well-documented being those foretelling the death of the dreamer or someone close to him or her. The citizens of ancient Rome seemed particularly fascinated by the possibility of this phenomenon and there are several reported instances of such dreams. For instance, the Roman historian Plutarch (AD 45-125) tells us that Calpurnia, the wife of Julius Caesar (100-44 BC), dreamed of Caesar's assassination by Brutus the night before it happened. Similarly the day before Caligula was assassinated, in AD 41, he reputedly dreamed that he was standing beside the heavenly throne of Jupiter, when the god gave him a push with his big toe, causing the emperor to fall to the earth.

DREAM DICTIONARIES

While the Greeks may have brought elements of logic and reason to the world of dreams, it took the orderly Romans to catalogue and classify the information. One of the most outstanding contributions was Artemidorus' five-volume *Oneirocritica* (The Interpretation of Dreams). A Roman soothsayer of the 2nd century AD,

Artemidorus travelled extensively throughout the Roman Empire, researching into dreams and drawing on knowledge from earlier times. His work includes more than 3000 dream reports from his interviewees, and is today acknowledged as the first true dream dictionary ever written.

Artemidorus suggests that dreams are entirely individual and that the contents are relevant only to the dreamer. The dream symbols and imagery that are found in these personal dreams are both cultural and individual, and are influenced by such aspects as the dreamer's health, state of mind and occupation. Artemidorus notes two broad classes of dreams: insomnium are dreams about everyday things and somnium are those that concerned the future. His approach is thorough and systematic and some symbolism is identified. For instance, dreaming of ploughing the earth is regarded as a sexual symbol, while a dream of a mouth represents the dreamer's home. More than a century later, a second *Oneirocriticon* appeared, compiled by Astrampsychus. This one contains such axiomatic statements as "to wear a purple robe threatens a lengthy disease".

ABOVE The assassination of Julius Caesar by Brutus was said to have been foreseen in a dream by his wife, Calpurnia. This detail of the story has survived, and has continued to fascinate people, from ancient Rome to modern times.

She dreamt tonight she saw my statue,
Which like a fountain with an hundred spouts
Did run pure blood; and many lusty Romans
Came smiling, and did bathe their hands in it.

WILLIAM SHAKESPEARE, JULIUS CAESAR

INDIA AND THE FAR EAST

WHILE THE CIVILIZATIONS OF THE NEAR AND MIDDLE EAST ATTRIBUTED DREAMS TO A DIVINE AGENT, IN INDIA AND THE FAR EAST THEY WERE REGARDED AS HAVING AN INNER SOURCE. IN CHINA DREAMS WERE THOUGHT TO EMANATE FROM THE SOUL, WHILE IN INDIA AND TIBET THEY WERE ASSOCIATED WITH A STATE OF MIND. IN ALL THESE CIVILIZATIONS, DREAMS WERE INEXTRICABLY LINKED WITH THE PHILOSOPHY, SPIRITUALITY AND MYTHOLOGY OF THEIR CULTURES. IN THE FAR EAST, IN PARTICULAR, SURVIVING TEXTS REVEAL A SOPHISTICATED UNDERSTANDING OF DREAMS, AN UNDERSTANDING ECHOED IN THE ORAL TRADITIONS OF MANY INDIGENOUS PEOPLES.

THE ATHARVA VEDA

According to legend, the 52 great Rishis (seers) of ancient India travelled to the highest mountains of the Himalayas seeking guidance to help humanity. During their meditations they believed that they discovered how the universe works. This knowledge was eventually transcribed into the Vedas, the sacred books of the Hindus, which scholars date between 1500-1000 BC. One of these texts, the *Atharva Veda*, contains many references to dreams, providing information about how they occur, what purpose they serve and how to interpret them.

LUCKY AND UNLUCKY DREAMS

When trying to make sense of complex information, a first response is often to classify it into opposites. This holds as true for dreams as for anything else. Where other ancient cultures distinguish between good and bad, divine or demonic, and true or false dreams, the Vedas focus on the distinction between "lucky" and "unlucky" dreams, having particular

interest in a dream's predictive power. For instance, the *Atharva Veda* comments that showing passivity in a dream is a bad omen, whereas an aggressive dream is favourable. However if the dreamer receives any injury, this is considered an ill omen. The omen is made worse if the injury, such as an amputation of a limb, is something that could occur in waking life. The effects of unlucky dreams can be countered by performing purification rites, such as burning incenses and ritual bathing.

TIMING AND PERSONALITY

For the first time, the personality type of the dreamer is taken into account in dream interpretation. For instance, a depressed person is more likely to have depressing dreams, while a hyperactive sort is more likely to have manic dreams. The *Atharva Veda* also theorizes that a person's dreams occur in cycles throughout the night, with the most important dreams occurring towards the end of the dreaming cycle or later on in

HINDU DEITIES

During the Vedic period a pantheon of Hindu deities developed. A lot of these gods and goddesses have strange, dream-like qualities to them. For instance, Ganesh is the elephant-headed god of wisdom and "remover of obstacles", and the god Shiva has four arms, four faces and three eyes. Shiva wears the skin of a tiger and has a snake entwined around his neck, representing two powerful demons that he has defeated. In his fight against a particularly powerful demon, Shiva calls on the goddess Kali, the "dark side" of his consort Devi, to help him. Kali (shown left) is usually depicted wearing a girdle of severed arms and a necklace of skulls. Her bloodthirsty tongue lolls from her mouth and she carries a sword in her left hand. Intoxicated by her murderous killings, she dances on the bodies of her victims.

the night. In fact the later on in the night a dream occurs, states the Vedas, the more likely, as well as the more quickly, it is to come true.

THE TWO WORLDS

The Vedas also contains texts known as the Upanishads, philosophical works that expose spiritual truths. One of the most elaborate and important of these is known as *Brihadaranyaka*, sometimes described as a "cosmic meditation". This text declares that essentially there are two states, one in this world and one in the other. A third intermediary state exists: the state of sleep and the land of dreams. It is while we are in the intermediary world that we have the capacity to perceive the real world and the next simultaneously. In this context, the dreaming state is considered to be more important than the waking state because it is then that we have access to realms of knowledge and experience denied to us when we are awake. To this end, techniques such as yoga and meditation were developed to help us "attain" or become more open to this other world, experienced as a place of heavenly bliss.

ABOVE The Hindus believe we can attain enlightenment during our dreams, only for it to evaporate when we wake.

ABOVE To the Buddhists this whole world is a waking dream. Once we perceive this we can really wake up to a new reality. But might not this also be another dream?

THE FAR EAST

It was not only in India that dreams were linked with spirituality and states of mind. An important Chinese Taoist manuscript, known as the Lie-tsu, distinguishes between six different types of dreaming: ordinary dreams, day-residue dreams, dreams of waking, dreams of fear, joyful dreams and terror dreams. Taoism, and later, Buddhism, were hugely influential throughout the Far East. Both of these spiritual traditions assert that the worlds we see in our dreams are more or less identical to the worlds we will experience after death.

THE BARDO

The Book of the Dead is an ancient Tibetan Buddhist text. Written to help prepare the soul for death, it describes death as a dream-like condition. When the soul leaves the physical body it must pass through the "Bardo", which has three distinct illusory states.

RIGHT The Tibetan Book of the Dead is a very ancient manuscript written on wooden tablets. In it a dialogue with the dead, who are said to have entered the bardo, the dream state between the living and the dead, is carried out.

As we pass through each state we face a multitude of self-created thought forms which may be pleasant or fearful, according to our thoughts and expectations. By becoming aware at any time that what we are experiencing is an illusion, the soul is elevated to a higher plane and avoids the constant cycle of death and rebirth. Consequently, learning to remain conscious while sleeping, being aware that we are dreaming while still in the dream, is seen by Tibetan Buddhists as a vital part of the spiritual preparation for death. Today in the West this state or technique is referred to as "lucid dreaming".

P'O AND HUN

In ancient China, it was believed that we possess two types of soul. The material soul, or "p'o" motivates us in daily life and is implicit in our physical make-up. This soul dies when the body dies. Additionally, we possess an eternal soul, or "hun", which survives us at death, leaving the physical body and the material world for a different plane of existence.

Every night during sleep, the hun temporarily separates from the dreamer's resting body to travel the world of dreams. This concept is similar to the idea many Western esoteric traditions hold today of the dream body and astral travel. As the dreamer sleeps, the hun communicates with spirits, demons and ghosts, bringing back memories of its nightly travels to the dreamer.

THE CITY OF DREAMS

In ancient China, people believed in a divine City of Dreams. Known as Ch'eng Huang, the city was thought to hang halfway between heaven and earth and is the place we go to when asleep. To enter the celestial city the dreamer had to pass through the "moongate", which necessitated being pure in mind and body. Once safely inside the city, the dreamer could leave their body and astral travel anywhere in the world. In this context, it is interesting to note that the Chinese had a god of the South Pole, a geographical region they had not actually discovered. Did the Chinese know of its existence because they had travelled there in their dreams?

BEDROOM RITUALS

To pass through the moongate easily, rituals were practised before going to sleep. These included lighting incense and proceeding around the bedroom in an anti-clockwise direction, beginning in the east and moving through south, west and north before getting into bed. It was also important to make sure the bedroom was decorated in auspicious colours (typically red and gold), and to make sure that nothing hung over the bed which could interfere with the exit of the spirit body. Consequently it was thought inadvisable to sleep under such things as beams, canopies, mirrors or lights. Similarly great care had to be taken to ensure that the spirit body could safely return to the dreamer's physical body. Playing tricks on a sleeping person, such as altering their physical appearance in some way, or else waking someone up too abruptly was believed to be dangerous. The returning soul needed to be able to recognize the sleeping body and it also needed time to re-enter the body. If the soul could not return for some reason, the sleeper would die.

ABOVE The Chinese believe that every part of the natural landscape is ruled by mythical creatures who protect it.
ABOVE LEFT The Chinese landscape has a dreamlike quality.

DREAMS AND ASTROLOGY

Written around AD 640, the earliest Chinese book of dream interpretations is the *Meng Shu*. It suggests that many factors should be taken into account before interpreting a dream. These include the time of year and astrological factors such as the position of the planets. It was also believed that external stimuli could be reflected in dreams. Sleeping on a belt, for instance, might produce dreams of a snake.

MU JEN DOLLS

In ancient China, great faith was placed in Mu Jen, the wooden man, or dream doll. For instance, if a child was suffering nightmares, the parents would "give" the dream to the Mu Jen doll, and he would then be sent away, taking the bad dream with him. Alternatively, if a dreamer wanted to make her wish come true, she would whisper it to the doll and then place him under her pillow as she slept. It was believed that during sleep the Mu Jen would come to life and be your "sacred warrior", capable of granting a person's wishes, protecting them from harm, and generally acting as a friend and helper.

EUROPEAN TRADITIONS

THE CUSTOM OF SLEEPING AT HOLY PLACES TO INCUBATE PARTICULAR DREAMS WAS NOT CONFINED TO THE ANCIENT AND CLASSICAL WORLD. THROUGHOUT EUROPE, THE PAGAN CELTS AND THE EARLY CHRISTIANS ALIKE PRACTISED THE SAME PROCEDURE, SLEEPING AT SHRINES TO ENCOURAGE VISIONS AND DREAMS OF HEALING POWER. FOR THE CELTS, THESE SACRED SPOTS WERE ASSOCIATED WITH NATURE SPIRITS, AND FOR THE CHRISTIANS WITH THE SAINTS AND MARTYRS OF THE EARLY CHURCH. AS THE INFLUENCE OF THE CHURCH BECAME MORE WIDESPREAD HOWEVER, DREAMS WERE REGARDED WITH INCREASED SUSPICION UNTIL, BY THE MIDDLE AGES, THEY WERE LARGELY SEEN AS THE DEVIL'S WORK.

CELTIC WISDOM

The Celts believed that all things possess an immortal soul, which exists through many lifetimes, learning from its experiences on the earthly plane in its journey towards perfection. To ascertain the will of the gods and help the soul along its way, many methods of prophecy and divination were used. The natural world was believed to be an infinite source of magic and spiritual wisdom, and symbolic significance was given to such things as the shape of clouds, a particular animal or plant species, as well as the portents of dreams. Dreams were interpreted by the druid, which literally means the "oak seer", or "one who sees with the aid of the oak". In fact, trees were especially important, and specific qualities were attributed to each species. Dreams were incubated in sacred groves, where the dreamer could ask the spirit of the trees for healing and assistance.

THE EARLY CHURCH

Traditional Celtic lore was frowned upon by Catholic doctrine, but theologians of the early Church also began to comment on their dreams. In his treatise *On the Making of Man* (380 AD), Gregory

BELOW RIGHT Dreams were part of the religious and artistic world of the Celts and artefacts from this era reflect this.
BELOW Dreams to early cultures were powerful messages from the gods, from nature, and from deep within. They were never to be ignored.

THE SALMON OF WISDOM
Stories about the source of all knowledge are practically universal. These symbolic tales have a rich, dream-like quality to them.

In the Irish Celtic tradition, the well of Nine Hazels is the dwelling place of the Salmon of Wisdom. The Salmon became wise when he imbibed the hazel nuts that fell into the well from the nine hazel trees. It is said that whoever catches and eats the salmon, will be imbued with its wisdom and filled with "imbas", or inspiration. Finn Eces, an elderly druid, captures the salmon and asks his young apprentice, Fionn mac Cumhail, to cook it for him. While it is cooking, some liquor from the fish splashes on to Fionn's thumb, and it is he and not Finn who gains the inspiration from the well.

of Nyssa asserts that dreams occur when the intellect and senses are at rest during sleep. The actual dream content is determined by the dreamer's memories of activities during waking life and his or her physical state. In other words, an individual's nature is revealed in his or her dreams. In Nyssa's view, dreams are most commonly motivated by the

passions, expressions of our "brute" nature which should be rigorously held in check by the intellect if we are to remain pure. Because the intellect is "off guard" during sleep, our passions can be given unbridled expression in our dreams. A little later, St Augustine (354-430 AD) noted that certain aspects of his mind were beyond his control, and he worried that God might hold him responsible for his dreams.

THE MIDDLE AGES

It was not long before the Christian Church associated human passions, especially sexual desires, with the devil or Satan. In their dreams, people were vulnerable to the temptations of the flesh: they could sin while asleep and not even know it, risking their souls to eternal damnation and the terrors of Hell. They therefore should practise great vigilance against the devil and all his works, as he was believed to intervene in human affairs in order to possess people's souls. A regime of devout prayer and austerity was recommended and any who continued to "sup with the devil" were branded as witches, facing persecution, torture and a terrible

death. Consequently the capacity to have vivid dreams was greatly feared and dream divination became linked with sorcery. It was at this point that dream divination in the West became anathema and consequently went underground, until its secular revival centuries later.

ABOVE Dreams are mysterious markers of landscapes that affect us very deeply – archetypes aren't just people but also symbolize aspects of ancient cultures.

TREE LORE

The Celts ascribed a symbolic meaning to trees. The oak, or "godhead" tree, held divine power and significance. Sleeping next to an oak tree could inspire prophetic dreams. Other important trees were the hazel, used as the druid's staff; holly, its red berries symbolizing the food of the gods; and ash, denoting health and immortal life.

THE DEVIL'S HELPERS

One of the dangers facing the dreamer was a nightly visitation from one of the devil's helpers. A succubus is a demon who assumes a female form and has sex with sleeping men. She then collects the semen, using it in magical rites to produce an "incubus", a male demon, satyr, faun or devil. Any man unfortunate, or some would say, wicked, enough to attract the attentions of a succubus was destined to follow the ways of the witch forever. By this means, Satan was said to "increase his horde, his progeny and to spread the diabolical craft of the witch".

THE SHEPHERD AND THE SUCCUBUS

The 16th-century author, Nicolas Remy, reports that a young shepherd who was found guilty of witchcraft began his evil ways by being seduced by a succubus while attending his flocks. It was said that whenever he fell asleep in the warm afternoon sunshine, he would dream of his demon lover, who took the form of a dairymaid with whom he was in love. She would allow the shepherd to fulfil his sexual desires with her provided that "he acknowledged her as his Mistress and behaved to her as though she were God Himself". The shepherd claimed that "she so possessed me that from that time I have been subject to no will but hers".

ABOVE Today we are much more forgiving of people who suffer or enjoy sexual excitement while asleep but to the ancient Church such people were very wicked indeed, and were inevitably accused of Devilish practices.

Witches, it was claimed, had sexual intercourse with incubi in order that they could give birth to the children of demons.

NOCTURNAL INTERCOURSE

The word "incubus" means "to lie on", and it was believed that any heavy feeling in bed, such as a weight pressing down on your chest, especially if accompanied by nightmares, was a sure sign that an incubus (or succubus) had attempted to have nocturnal intercourse with you. Today we know that dreaming affects the body as well as the brain. For both men and women, the body regularly shows signs of sexual arousal (sometimes to the point of orgasm) during sleep, even when erotic dream content is absent. Given the religious fervour of the Middle Ages, it is not altogether surprising that the idea of a demon lover was believed to account for this phenomenon.

FORERUNNERS OF THE MODERN AGE

Although St Augustine was concerned about his inability to control his dreams, it was hundreds of years later before the idea that something goes on inside us that we know nothing about was clearly formulated. Von Leibniz (1646-1716) compared the workings of the soul to the circulation of blood through the body: it is something that happens even though we are unaware of it. A little later, a German physicist, G.C. Lichtenberg (1742-99) made the first link between unconscious mental activity and dreaming.

At the beginning of the 19th century, signs of a renewed interest in dreams began to gather momentum. Robert Cross Smith from England became very successful as an astrologer, practising under the pseudonym of "Raphael". In 1830, he published *The Royal Book of Dreams,* which gave the reader interpretations of particular kinds of dream. However, it is through the work of a French doctor, Alfred Maury (1817-1892), that we begin to enter a new age of dream interpretation. From his study of more than 3000 dreams, Maury concludes that external stimuli are often responsible for what we dream about. Recent memories appearing in dreams, especially of the day before, are referred to as "day residues", and Maury discovered that stimuli such as noises and smells often register as we sleep and become included in our dreams.

ABOVE RIGHT Much of the accusations levelled against so called witches by the Church involved detailed, nightmarish descriptions of the devilish creatures the women were said to have under their control.
RIGHT The only way to redeem a witch or possessed person was to exorcise the malignant spirit and extract a confession from the accused.

MAURY'S DREAM

In one of his dreams, Maury dreamt he had been condemned to death by the guillotine. As the blade was falling, he woke up to find the top of the bed had fallen and hit him on the back of the neck at the exact time the guillotine would have struck him. This gave weight to Maury's theory that dreams happen so quickly that they are almost concurrent with the external stimulus that produces them.

THE DREAM DEMON OF MORAY FIRTH

Legend has it that in the 16th century, a demon lover lived near the banks of the Moray Firth River in Scotland. The lover seduces a young girl, but the lovers are caught when the girl's parents overhear sounds of lovemaking coming from her bedchamber. The parents call the priest and together break down the bedchamber door to find the girl fast asleep in the embrace of a "monster horrible beyond description". The priest recites from the gospels, whereupon the evil demon gives a terrible cry, setting fire to the furniture in the room and vanishing upwards, carrying the roof of the bedchamber with him.

INDIGENOUS PEOPLES

TRADITIONAL SOCIETIES ACROSS THE GLOBE HAVE DREAMING TRADITIONS THAT STRETCH BACK INTO THE MISTS OF TIME. IT SEEMS THAT DREAMS HAVE ALWAYS BEEN PART OF THE FABRIC OF LIFE FOR PEOPLES AS DIVERSE AS THE AUSTRALIAN ABORIGINES, THE INUIT FROM THE ARCTIC REGIONS AND THE PEOPLES OF AFRICA, AS WELL AS THE NATIVE AMERICAN INDIANS. EACH CULTURE HAS ITS OWN THEORY OF DREAMING AND PARTICULAR TECHNIQUES FOR INTERPRETING DREAMS. THEIR DREAMS AND SYMBOLS RELATE TO A PARTICULAR WAY OF LIFE, YET THEY ALL HAVE SOMETHING IN COMMON. THEIR DREAMS ARE RESPECTED AS COMING FROM A REVERED SOURCE AND ARE SEEN TO CONTAIN IMPORTANT INFORMATION.

ABOVE To the Aborigines of Australasia nothing is more sacred, more important, or more meaningful than the dreamtime, when the world was first created out of the seeds of the spirit ancestors.

THE DREAMTIME

Hundreds of thousands of years ago, the Aborigines travelled from Asia to the northern shores of Australia. Here they split into groups and moved around the land in search of water. They travelled great distances, and their legends say that as they did so they deposited the spirits of those yet to be born along the way, leaving marks on the landscape, on the rocks, mountains and other geographical features, to signpost the places they had been. According to legend, these ancestors were mythical figures, spirit beings who emerged from the earth, sea and sky and who took on various forms, particularly of animals. They were given symbolic names such as Red Kangaroo, the Blue Lizard or the Bell Bird Brothers. This era is known as the "dreamtime", when the ancestors created the landscape and set the pattern for the future. For centuries the Australian Aborigines have followed in the footsteps of their ancestors, tracing the paths trodden by these giant beings and marking their sacred sites with ritual, song and legend.

Those who lose dreaming are lost.   AUSTRALIAN ABORIGINAL PROVERB

The dreamtime is like a "cosmic dreaming energy" which can be set free if the ground is rubbed or stroked at the exact spot where the ancestor left the world at death and went into the ground. In ritual dances, these sacred sites on the landscape are struck and the power of the ancestors is brought back to life from the sleep of death. If no-one remembers or honours the dreamtime, the stories say, we shall remain trapped in the earth when we die and will cease to be.

THE DREAM IS LIFE

The dreamtime of the Aborigines is a complex concept: it is at once a creation myth, a whole series of fables and an entire spiritual philosophy. For the native Australians, the whole of life had its evolution in the dreamtime, and for them everything around us is brought to life by the dream. They do not perceive time as a linear process but rather see humans as existing in an eternal "now", where past, present and future exist simultaneously. The world as they see it is a magical place imbued with

supernatural forces, and we are at all times "dreaming the dream" so that it can become impossible to differentiate between the waking and the dreaming state.

AFRICAN SOCIETIES

The Bushmen of the Kalahari hold a similar viewpoint, seeing the whole of life as a dream and believing that they are the ones being "dreamed". Similarly, the Pagiboti people of Zaire consider that dreams are sent from their ancestors and believe that the spirits of the past have access to wisdom that can help with daily life. For instance, hunting is important to the survival of the Pagiboti and they believe their dreams can give them important information that can help them be successful: to dream of encountering an animal in the forest is regarded as a good sign. Many other African societies set great store by dreams, believing that they are linked to destiny. All aspects of life, from cures for sickness to political decisions, can be based on dream advice.

ABOVE According to the Aborigine creation myths we are all holders of the dreamtime.
ABOVE LEFT The Aborigines' sacred art consists of pictorial representations of the dreamtime and how the world was created.

THE DREAM SMOKE OF ULURU

The two Bell Bird Brothers were hunting emu at the rock pool near Uluru, the most sacred of all Australian Aboriginal sites (right), when their prey was disturbed by a young girl eating grubs. On her head she carried a sacred bundle which fell to the ground – the indentation is still to be seen at the base of the rock – but the brothers managed to catch the emu. They killed it and cooked it but Blue Lizard came and stole it. In punishment the Bell Bird Brothers set fire to Blue Lizard's hut and he was burned alive. The smoke from the fire can still be seen across the face of Uluru, and it is the smoke from this fire that sets us dreaming.

This story indicates one of the reasons why Uluru is so important to the Australian Aborigines. Take the rock out of their control and they lose their power of dreaming, and by implication, the power to live.

NORTH AMERICAN INDIAN TRADITIONS

Like other traditional societies, Native American cultures find it difficult to define the border between the waking and the dreaming state, and the ability to dream is highly valued. Each of the great tribes has its own understanding of dreams and a complex dream culture exists. Iroquois traditionalists, for instance, have a strong belief in dream precognition and respect the ability of a gifted dreamer to provide information vital to the survival of the people. Because Iroquois culture is built on warrior values, any sign of being taken care of in a dream is greatly feared, as it is believed that it will undermine

ABOVE LEFT Through dream journeys the shaman is able to connect with the animal world.
ABOVE RIGHT The shaman is the guide through the dream. Without the shaman our dreams are dangerous places to go.

bravery. Where a dream indicates trouble or disaster, it is believed to be possible to change its outcome by playacting the event that the community wishes to avert. In fact drama and ritual play an important part in Iroquois dream culture. Each year people travel great distances to attend a festival where dreams are acted out in a theatrical performance known as the *Ondinnonk*. According to the Iroquois, big dreams occur either because we have an out-of-body experience during sleep or because we receive an interesting "dream visitor". These are the dreams that put us in touch with our deepest spiritual source and contain vital information for health and wellbeing.

The Navajo pay particular attention to the diagnostic aspect of dreams, seeing them as tools to pinpoint illness, particular mental states and emotional disturbances. Dreams can also reveal a ritual cure for what is wrong, and if this is carried out in waking life the dreamer will return to health. For instance, there is a story of a sick girl

LEFT Ritual dances can be followed to interpret the dream in song and music. This is a valuable tool in dream interpretation but one that is specific to a culture, to those who understand the steps.

THE FOUR DIRECTIONS

Each of the four directions is associated with a particular element and quality. The element of the North is air. North is associated with the power of the mind and clear-thinking. Water belongs to the South and is associated with feelings and intuition, while the power of the West revitalizes and renews the physical body. Its element is earth. The power of the East triggers enlightenment and spiritual realization and its element is fire. This Navajo sand painting uses the four elements in its symbolic representation of abundant crops.

It is believed that positioning the bed in a particular direction allows the dreamer to "work" with the qualities of its associated element.

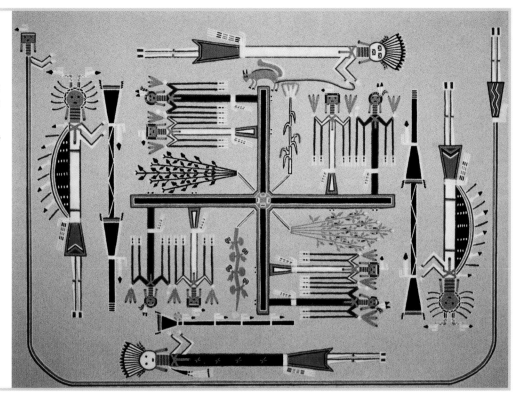

dreaming of nine feasts and being persuaded by the medicine man that if she has these feasts in reality, she would recover from her illness.

HOPI DREAM PROMPTERS

For the Hopi, a dream is viewed as a message from spirit guides who can appear in the form of an animal or other guises. Waking up and not remembering a dream is seen as losing something essential and people go to great lengths to ensure that this does not happen.

A commonly used dream prompter is a squared circle, a symbolic device used to aid dream recall. A circle is drawn on a square piece of cloth or leather. The circle is then divided into four quarters to represent each of the four directions: North, South, West and East. The square is then placed by the side of the bed. An item of symbolic value is placed in each of the four quarters – for instance, a tiny pot of water, a bunch of fresh grass, a lit candle and some burning incense – these items represent each of the four elements of water, earth, fire and air. Sleeping next to a dream prompter is believed to enhance dream recall.

THE INUIT SHAMAN

The Canadian Inuit culture is similar to those found in other northern regions, such as in Russia and the northern Scandinavian countries, where survival is challenged by the extreme climate. The Inuit believe that *anua* (souls) exist in all people and animals. Individuals, families and the tribe follow a system of taboos to ensure that animals will continue to make themselves available to the hunters, and rituals and ceremonies are performed before and after hunting expeditions to encourage success.

The shaman is the spiritual leader of each tribe. He is able to interpret causes of sickness or lack of success in hunting. In a manner similar to shamans or medicine-men in other cultures, he enters a trance-like state with the aid of drum beating and chanting. This allows him to travel out of his body, traversing great distances to determine the causes of sickness and other community problems, and to bring back solutions. In this dream-like state the shaman is imbued with magical powers and can move about outside of the dream.

CULTURAL PATTERN DREAMS

Anthropologists have suggested that the dreams of traditional societies can be broken down into four types: "big" dreams are those that possess cultural significance; prophetic dreams predict or give advance warning of events; medical dreams promote diagnosis and healing; and "little" dreams are purely personal to the dreamer. Although all dreams are valued, the ones held to be the most significant are the big dreams. These powerful dreams are also known as "cultural pattern dreams" or "official dreams".

The dream world is the real world. SENECA INDIAN HEALER

SACRED DREAMING

THROUGHOUT THE ANCIENT WORLD, THE CONNECTION BETWEEN DREAMS AND SPIRITUAL BELIEF WAS CLOSELY INTERWOVEN. DREAMS SEEM TO HAVE PLAYED A SIGNIFICANT ROLE IN THE SHAPING OF MANY OF THE WORLD'S MAJOR RELIGIONS, APPEARING AS PART OF THEIR HISTORY AND IN THEIR HOLY TEXTS. MANY OF THESE DREAMS HAVE A REVELATORY OR VISIONARY QUALITY TO THEM, WITH RICH SYMBOLIC IMAGERY AND METAPHOR. THESE EXPERIENCES ARE NOT THE SAME AS THE ORDINARY DREAMS MOST OF US HAVE MUCH OF THE TIME — ALTHOUGH IT IS POSSIBLE TO EXPERIENCE A DREAM OF SUCH PROFOUND SIGNIFICANCE THAT LIFE CAN NEVER BE THE SAME AGAIN.

BUDDHIST ENLIGHTENMENT

For a long time before the birth of Gautama Buddha (c.563-c.483 BC), many predictions had been made that a "chosen one" would arrive. While she was pregnant, Gautama's mother dreamt that she was carrying a shining, silvery white elephant with six tusks. Interpreters regarded the dream as an announcement of the chosen one's arrival. Elephants had holy status in India: the Hindu god, Ganesh, remover of obstacles, is depicted with an elephant's head, while the unusual colour and appearance of the elephant in the dream was also seen as significant. Later on in the Buddha's life, his father, a nobleman, had a dream in which his son left the family to become a monk. This came to pass when Gautama was 30 years old, when he left his family, renouncing his worldly status to seek enlightenment.

BIBLICAL VISIONS

Dreams also figure largely in both the Old and New Testaments. In the Old Testament, important dreams often coincide with critical times in the development of Judaism. For instance, while in exile in Egypt Joseph interprets the Pharaoh's dreams. The Pharaoh

BELOW Gabriel, a universal archetype who appears in several different traditions, played a significant part in the dreams of Mohammed, who dreamt that they journeyed together to the seven levels of heaven.

HINDU BELIEFS

The Hindu religion has its own interpretation of what dreams are all about and believes that some dreams come from the dreamer's own emotional nature, some from hidden fears, and some from playing back experiences in daily life. Certain dreams, however, come from the gods. These dreams only appear to very religious people, such as this sadhu (right), who live a disciplined life, or sadhana, getting up before sunrise and practising austerities.

And He said, 'Hear now my words: If there be a prophet among you, I the lord will make myself known unto him in a vision and will speak to him in a dream'. OLD TESTAMENT, NUMBERS 12:6

RIGHT Joseph became a dream interpreter to the Pharaoh, and in this role became one of the most important people in the land. The Egyptians believed that dreams were messages from the gods.

dreams that seven fat cattle are eaten by seven lean ones, and then that seven ripe ears of corn are destroyed by seven blighted ones. Joseph realizes that both dreams mean the same thing: they predict seven years of plentiful harvest followed by seven years of scarcity, which will destroy the bounty of the previous seven years. The Pharaoh acts on Joseph's interpretation and during the bounteous years builds up large stores of grain. The interpretation not only saves the populace and the ruling system, but Joseph is promoted to a position of great political influence.

In the New Testament, divine messages are often relayed in dreams. The angel Gabriel appears in a vision to the pregnant Mary, announcing that she will give birth to a child of the Holy Spirit. The angel also visits Joseph in a dream, telling him to accept Mary's pregnancy and to name the baby Jesus, because he will save his people from their sins. Dreams also contain warnings. For instance, Joseph is told to take his family to Egypt in order to escape Herod's jurisdiction that all newborn male infants should be slain. Later the same angel returns to Joseph, informing him that it is safe to return after Herod is dead.

ISLAMIC DREAMS

Dreams also seem to have played an important part in the building of Islam. It is said that Mohammed (c.570-632 AD) had visions of the archangel Gabriel, who appeared to him when he was alone at night, praying and meditating. During one such

THE TALMUD

The body of Jewish civil and ceremonial law, the Talmud, divides dreams into three types: dreams of prophecy, dreams of nonsense, and dreams that originate from a person's thoughts and experience during the day. The way a dream is interpreted helps determine its outcome, and actions such as fasting or reciting special prayers are recommended as atonement for a bad dream.

visitation, the angel dictated the first chapter, or Sura, of the Koran, the holy book of Islam. The Arabic root for the word *Koran* means "address" or "recitation". According to tradition, Mohammed could neither read nor write, but the Koran was recited word by word by him just as he had received it from Gabriel. Later Mohammed had a dream or vision that he journeyed in the company of Gabriel and other angels. He was taken to holy places and to the seven levels of heaven and hell, meeting important religious leaders and prophets from the past. This experience, referred to as the Night Journey, has inspired many writers and artists.

ABOVE Angels have appeared to many in dreams, are these dreams or visions? Moments of madness or divine communications? One of the most well known angelic dreams is Mary's, as she is told of the coming of Jesus.

THE NATURE OF DREAMS

A dream is a series of pictures or events that occur in the mind. Generally dreams are experienced as we sleep, although it is possible to enter a dream-like state while awake. These images seem to be based on the dreamer's thoughts or experiences although certain dreams seem to bear little or no relation to the dreamer's normal life. Precisely how and why these images occur and what relevance they may have is a subject that has inspired a great deal of research and provokes much debate.

In this section we shall explore the nature of dreams, looking at some of the most influential ideas from science and psychology, drawing particularly on the work of Freud and Jung. Some modern approaches to dreaming are discussed before going on to investigate paranormal phenomena, dream travel and out-of-body experiences. Other dream states in the "twilight zone" are examined before finishing with a look at lucid dreaming. Although we may not have one single, comprehensive theory about dreaming, there can be few who would deny it is a fascinating subject.

SCIENTIFIC RESEARCH

THE RELATIONSHIP BETWEEN THE BODY AND MIND, THE BRAIN AND SLEEP HAS ALWAYS BEEN A PUZZLE, YET SCIENTIFIC RESEARCH INTO DREAMS IS A RELATIVELY RECENT PHENOMENON. EARLY RESEARCH IN THE 19TH CENTURY SUGGESTED THAT EXTERNAL STIMULI, SUCH AS NOISES AND SMELLS, CAN INFLUENCE DREAM CONTENT AND CERTAIN DREAM EXPERIENCES WERE GIVEN A PHYSIOLOGICAL EXPLANATION. HOWEVER IT WAS NOT UNTIL THE PHYSICS OF ELECTRICITY WAS UNDERSTOOD AND EEG (ELECTROENCEPHALOGRAM) INSTRUMENTS WERE INVENTED THAT SCIENTISTS BEGAN TO DISCOVER HOW THE BRAIN WORKS, TRANSFORMING OUR KNOWLEDGE OF SLEEP AND DREAMS.

EEG INVESTIGATIONS

In the early 1950s at the University of Chicago, Kleitman and Aserinsky made a breakthrough in sleep research using EEGs. They found that when a person was asleep the brain had periods of intense activity, demolishing the widespread idea that during sleep the brain was resting. They also found out that blind people have vivid dreams in colour.

Another important dream researcher was Kleitman's pupil, William Dement, to whom we owe the term "REM (rapid eye movement) sleep". REM occurs after periods of slow-wave or deep sleep, at regular intervals throughout the night. REM is characterized by visibly detectable movements of the eye behind closed eyelids together with a change in brainwave frequency. It is during REM sleep that we experience dreams.

Dement's research team found that if someone is woken in or immediately after REM sleep they usually have good recall of their dreams. On the other hand, if even as little as five minutes has elapsed before they wake, they usually have little or no memory of their dreams.

PHASIC AND TONIC DREAMS

We now know that REM sleep falls into two types, generating two different types of dreams. Firstly there is the phasic component. This is characterized by jerky eye movements, spasmodic limb and facial twitching and sudden breathing changes. When volunteers are woken from this sort of REM sleep, they typically describe their dreams as being strongly visual, active and "real". Phasic REM and its accompanying dreams tend to occur later on in the sleeping period. Nightmares are associated with this type of sleep.

The second type of REM sleep is known as tonic and is accompanied by muscle relaxation and

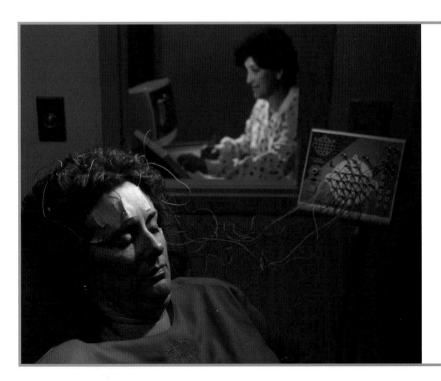

PHASIC AND TONIC DREAMS

REM sleep has two components, each having its own dream characteristics.

phasic dream I was running down a metal tunnel. It was very cold and hard and my feet made a noise on the floor as I ran. There were vibrant colours inside the tunnel and I felt I could reach out and touch them. Behind me I could hear the echoing roar of rushing water and it made me tremble. I wasn't afraid but I did feel very anxious – you know the sort of feeling, where you think the worst is going to happen at any minute. It was pretty overpowering.

tonic dream I was sitting in a temple meditating. There was a monk beside me and I could sense what he was thinking. There was a feeling of calm and peace all around and I drifted away in the swirling incense smoke. I felt weightless and insubstantial.

sometimes sexual arousal. Tonic REM takes place earlier on in the sleeping cycle. It is calmer and more restful, and tonic dreams are more passive and "feely". When woken, the dreamer typically reports such things as "I was feeling floaty" or "there was a feeling of peace".

DATA THEORIES

Although we now know much more about the brain, scientists remain divided as to the exact purpose that dreaming serves. In the 1960s, some dream researchers thought that while we are asleep the brain, like a computer, is "off-line". This does not mean it has shut down, but is that is going through a process of reassessing, filing and updating data from the day's activities. Many dreams certainly seem to fall into this category.

Some researchers took the analogy even further by suggesting that the brain, like the computer, discards redundant information through the process of dreaming. In the 1980s, Crick and Mitchison called this process "reverse learning". Dreams, they reasoned, help the mind to jettison an overload of data which could otherwise cause confusion. Dreams are like a rubbish-bin of the mind and have no particular meaning. From this perspective, we dream in order to forget.

UNDERSTANDING THE BRAIN

The brain has two hemispheres: the left side is associated with logic and language, while the right is more connected with intuition and creativity. It seems that dreaming is associated with right brain activity. Scientists have also discovered that dreams flow along visual and verbal "pathways" or nerve channels to the brain. We also know that the brain emits different types of electrical signals or waves. Of these, the following four types are of interest to sleep researchers. Beta waves (30-13 hertz) are associated with normal waking activity, with waves near the top end of the scale (30) signalling states of extreme agitation. Alpha waves (12-8 hertz) are produced during rest, while theta waves (7-5 hertz) are produced on the point of sleep. Delta waves are the longest and slowest (4-1 hertz) and are produced during deep sleep or in the womb. It is usually when alpha moves into theta that dreaming begins.

ABOVE The more we understand the function of the brain the better able we are to understand our dreams and thus not only our emotional impulses but also, perhaps, our spiritual function.

BELOW LEFT Our dreams may be a simple way of us downloading all the data we have picked up during the day and may have no meaning at all.
BELOW On the other hand dreams may be imbued with mystical importance and we would be lost without them – lesser beings indeed.

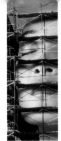

FREUDIAN PSYCHOLOGY

WHILE PEOPLE HAVE ALWAYS BEEN INTERESTED IN THE WAY THE MIND WORKS, IT WAS NOT UNTIL THE 20TH CENTURY THAT OUR UNDERSTANDING WAS REVOLUTIONIZED. THIS BREAKTHROUGH CAN BE ATTRIBUTED TO THE WORK OF SIGMUND FREUD (1856-1939), AN AUSTRIAN NEUROLOGIST AND THE FOUNDER OF PSYCHOANALYSIS. FREUD "DISCOVERED" THE UNCONSCIOUS AND DESCRIBED DREAMS AS THE "ROYAL ROAD" TO ITS UNDERSTANDING. WHEN HIS *INTERPRETATION OF DREAMS* WAS PUBLISHED IN 1900 IT WAS HIGHLY CONTROVERSIAL, YET HIS IDEAS PERMEATED ALMOST EVERY ASPECT OF WESTERN CULTURE. BECAUSE OF FREUD, DREAMS WERE ONCE AGAIN TAKEN SERIOUSLY.

THE CONSCIOUS AND THE UNCONSCIOUS MIND

According to Sigmund Freud, the conscious part of the mind represents a small fraction of the whole. It is like the tip of the iceberg, with the unconscious lying below the surface of the water. Like the iceberg, part of the unconscious is near the water's surface. Freud refers to this level as the "pre-conscious" and it is relatively easy to get in touch with. The deeper levels, however, are more difficult to access. It is a journey into the dark.

The unconscious is not static but dynamic. Freud believed that underneath our social exterior, the tip of the iceberg, at rock bottom we are a seething mass of instincts and unspeakable desires, most of which relate to sexuality and aggression, or our biological drives. He refers to this part of the psyche as the "id". Any experiences, thoughts or desires that are either too painful to allow, or that will contradict our self-image are either denied by the rational, conscious part of the personality (referred to as the "ego"), or repressed by an internal "censor" (also known as the "superego"). The unconscious is a bubbling cauldron of our personal and social taboos, yet it also provides the underlying motivations for our behaviour, of which we are largely unaware.

THE ROLE OF DREAMS

Freud believed that the unconscious cannot be studied directly but can only be inferred from clues in a person's behaviour, speech patterns and also their dreams. Dreams are symbolic representations of our unconscious needs, wishes and conflicts. Freud describes them as being in essence "the hallucinatory fulfilment of a forbidden wish". He asserts that dreams not only represent current wishes but are also the irrational expressions of infantile wishes, usually of either a sexual or an aggressive nature, that are left over in our subconscious from early childhood.

Because the wish is perceived as dangerous by the censor, it is expressed in the dream in a disguised or symbolic form. Freud believed dreams have two aspects: a latent content (the repressed desire) and a manifest content (the dream itself). So, for instance, repression of sexual desires (latent content) leads us to dream in metaphors of sexual imagery (manifest content): to dream of a chimney is to dream of an erect penis, to dream of a cave is to dream of a vagina. In other words, dream symbols are coded

BELOW Sigmund Freud was the first modern Western scientist to make a detailed attempt to understand and interpret dreams, and his legacy continues to this day.

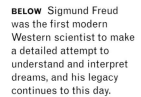

Anyone who behaved while awake in the way the situations in the dream present him would be regarded as insane.

SIGMUND FREUD

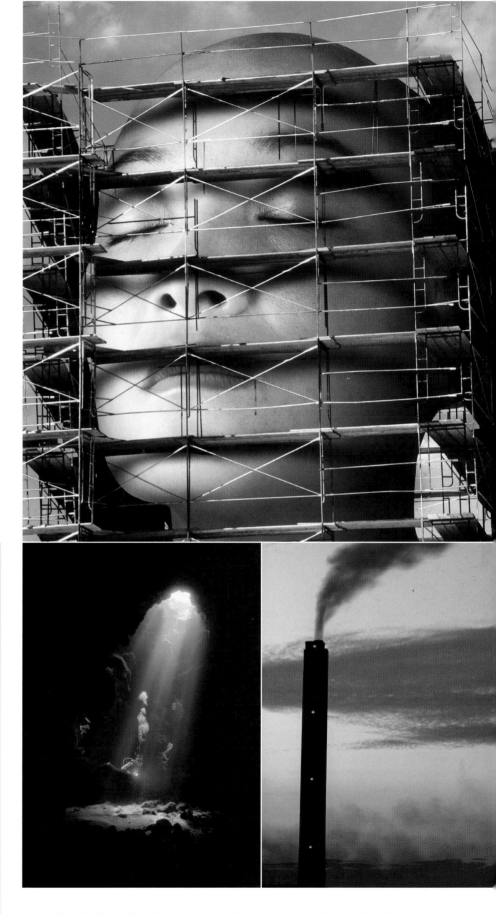

RIGHT Freud believed that dreams mask what is really going on in our subconscious, and we have to strip away the scaffolding to discover the true, to him invariably sexual, meaning of the dream.

messages, having sufficient ingenuity to slip through the tight webbing of the censor's net. Freud believed that this subversive activity was necessary because it allowed the sleeper to go on sleeping. Without such disguise techniques, the content would be so disturbing that the dreamer would be woken from sleep. This leads to Freud's description of dreams as "the guardians of sleep and not its disturbers".

APPROACH TO INTERPRETATION

Freud's approach to dream interpretation is to look for the underlying meaning, or the latent content, behind the dream. To help his patients identify the latent content of their dreams, Freud developed the technique of word association, known as "free association", where words and ideas derived from the dream are freely associated without being censored. This technique forms the basic method of psychoanalysis.

DREAM DISGUISES

Central to Freud's theory is that dreams use "disguise" techniques to hide the latent content from the internal censor. This is how he accounts for the peculiar and irrational nature of the manifest dream. These are the different disguise techniques that Freud identifies:

Condensation dreams use a kind of shorthand, coalescing or "condensing" different ideas together into a single image which is often unusual or bizarre.

Displacement dreams are when a potentially disturbing idea is redirected or "displaced" on to another person or object so that it becomes less disturbing. For instance, a young man harbours feelings of murderous rage towards his father. In his dream, he sees his father being killed by a stranger, whereby his aggressive desires are displaced on to the stranger.

Symbolization dreams are where a neutral image is used to represent a potentially disturbing, usually sexual, idea. For instance, putting a key into a keyhole is interpreted as a penis entering a vagina.

Representation dreams are when thoughts are converted into visual imagery.

ABOVE Freud believed that all dream imagery is symbolic in content, and that the symbolism is universal rather than personal. For example if you dream of holes in the ground, tunnels or caves (above left) you are dreaming about the vagina. Similarly, if you dream of chimneys or towers (right) you are dreaming of the penis.

PSYCHOLOGY AND JUNG

FOR OUR CONTEMPORARY UNDERSTANDING OF DREAM INTERPRETATION WE ARE INDEBTED TO THE WORK OF CARL GUSTAV JUNG (1875-1961), A SWISS PSYCHIATRIST AND FOUNDER OF "ANALYTICAL PSYCHOLOGY", WHO MADE THE STUDY OF DREAMS AND THE UNCONSCIOUS HIS LIFEWORK. JUNG WAS A ONE-TIME PUPIL OF FREUD, AND WAS IN AGREEMENT ABOUT THE IMPORTANCE OF UNCONSCIOUS PROCESSES IN THE CAUSE AND TREATMENT OF MENTAL ILLNESS AND IN THE PRODUCTION OF DREAMS. GRADUALLY HOWEVER, JUNG BECAME DISSATISFIED WITH FREUD'S THEORIES AND PROPOSED THAT DREAMS PLAYED AN IMPORTANT PART IN THE HEALTHY FUNCTIONING OF THE PSYCHE.

JUNG'S BASIC PHILOSOPHY

It was Freud's emphasis on sexuality and the overly biological orientation of his theories that gradually alienated his pupil, Jung. Freud's is a deterministic, and some would say, pessimistic, view of human behaviour. In a sense, he argues, we are little more than machines, driven by blind forces arising from our biological inheritance, over which we have little or no control. In contrast, Jung believed that human beings possess the capacity for growth and fulfilment and regarded sexual energy as part of a much more general, innate drive towards psychic health and wholeness. Jung calls this process individuation and describes it as the most important task any person can undertake in life – the attainment of harmony between all the aspects of the psyche, which makes us one and whole.

Essentially Jung saw life in terms of a spiritual journey and, far from being a dangerous melting pot of repressed and forbidden wishes, he saw the unconscious as a friend and guide to help us on our way. Jung applied these principles to his own life and used his dreams to help him make decisions, resolve uncertainties and move him along his path to self-realization.

THE PURPOSE OF DREAMS

Jung saw the psyche as self-adjusting, helping us to reconcile opposing parts of our nature and restore inner balance, and believed that dreams had an important part to play in this process. Dreams have a compensatory function, alerting us to imbalances in our personality and allowing us to change. They also have a teaching function, where certain aspects of the personality that need revising can be given attention. Jung believed that dreams are a way of communicating, of bringing levels of unconscious information into conscious awareness. They express the current state of the dreamer's unconscious and, Jung believed, they also provide clues as to future potential – a view that contrasts with Freud's more backward-looking perspective.

APPROACH TO INTERPRETATION

Unlike Freud, Jung never published a systematic theory of dream analysis because he believed that every dream carried its own meaning and must be interpreted individually. For Jung, the dream itself is the content and its symbols are subject to subjective interpretation. Rather than leading the person away from the dream by free association, Jung's method is to stay focused on the content of the dream itself. Through amplification or "direct association" he

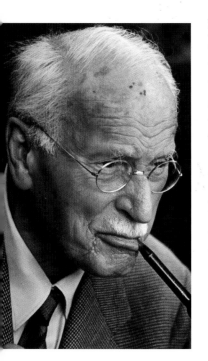

BELOW During his life, Jung estimated that he interpreted around 80,000 dreams. He found that the details of a dream were not only relevant to the dreamer, but were sometimes part of a bigger picture relating to the world we live in.

JUNG'S DREAM OF HIS FATHER

Following a dream of his dead father, Jung became interested in the spiritual dimension to life.

"Six weeks after his death, my father appeared to me in a dream. Suddenly he stood before me and said that he was coming back from his holiday. He had made a good recovery and was now coming home. I thought he would be annoyed with me for having moved into his room. But not a bit of it! Nevertheless, I felt ashamed because I had imagined he was dead. Two days later the dream was repeated. My father had recovered and was coming home, and again I reproached myself because I had thought he was dead. Later I kept asking myself: 'What does it mean that my father returns in dreams and that he seems so real?' It was an unforgettable experience and it forced me for the first time to think about life after death."

encourages the dreamer to explore all their associations with a particular image, returning to the image itself again and again.

THE COLLECTIVE UNCONSCIOUS

The other important area where Jung diverges from Freud is in the way he conceptualized the unconscious. Although many dreams are expressions of a personal unconscious and related to the individual psyche of the dreamer, Jung noticed that there were other dreams that do not fit into this category. These make use of symbols which have no particular personal significance for the dreamer, but have a "universal" quality about them. Through his studies of religion, art, anthropology and mythology, he concludes that many of these symbols stem from some common source – the "collective unconscious" the largest and deepest area of the psyche. He refers to these universal symbols as "archetypes" and argues that their meaning transcends the personal.

ABOVE To understand our personal archetypes is to unlock the power of our dreams and to be truly released.
ABOVE LEFT Jung encourages the dreamer to explore their own dream, and discover its meaning for themselves.

LEFT Archetypes can be traced back thousands of generations, and traces may even be seen in the landscape, where the first human cultures in our history drew the creatures of their imaginations.

MODERN APPROACHES

FOLLOWING IN THE FOOTSTEPS OF FREUD AND JUNG, THERE HAVE BEEN MANY OTHERS WHO HAVE DEVELOPED THEIR OWN METHODS OF USING DREAMS TO GAIN INSIGHT INTO THE INNER WORKINGS OF THE MIND. TODAY A MORE ECLECTIC APPROACH TOWARDS DREAM INTERPRETATION HAS GENERALLY BECOME ESTABLISHED AND A MIXTURE OF TECHNIQUES AND IDEAS IS IN USE. IN GENERAL TERMS, THE EMPHASIS IS ON THE DREAMER RATHER THAN THE DREAM, WITH EACH PERSON LEARNING HOW TO APPRECIATE AND INTERPRET THEIR OWN DREAMS. OUR DREAMS CAN HELP US LOOK AT THINGS FROM A NEW PERSPECTIVE OR EXAMINE NEGLECTED AREAS OF OURSELVES.

ABOVE Nowadays everything in our dreams is regarded as deeply symbolic – no tiny detail gets overlooked.
ABOVE RIGHT We like to think that everything in our dream can be explained – interpreted as being connected to our waking life in some way.

DREAM THEORISTS

The 20th century saw a revival of interest in dreams and a great deal of academic and scientific research into the subject was undertaken. Calvin Hall and his associate Vernon Nordby spent most of the 1950s and 60s collecting and categorizing dreams from all over the world.

After analysing more than 50,000 dreams Hall and Nordby concluded that typical themes crop up in dreams again and again, which seemed to lend weight to Jung's theory of the collective unconscious. They also rejected Freud's distinction between the latent and manifest content of dreams, believing that the dream itself was the message.

In the 1960s, Thomas French and Erika Fromm asserted that the primary function of dreams is to work on relationship issues in the dreamer's life, an approach that has proved extremely influential. Montague Ullman took French and Fromm's ideas a stage further by making a link between dreaming and cultural and social issues, asserting that in some way our dreams are concerned with our "interconnectedness" as a species.

EXPERIENTIAL APPROACHES

In recent times, experiential approaches to dreams have been favoured over those that are theory driven. In the 1960s Frederick (Fritz) Perls, the founder of Gestalt psychotherapy, emphasized the importance of taking all aspects of the dream as a direct expression of the personal psychology of the dreamer. His greatest contribution is his use of role-playing techniques to bring the different "parts" of the dream to greater consciousness. For instance in a dream of steering a ship, you would role-play "being" the ship as well as yourself, setting up a dialogue between the two aspects of the dream.

In the 1980s, Alvin Mahrer developed a four-part experiential model for working with dreams. First tell the dream, next identify recent events, situations or experiences connected with the dream, go on to re-experience peak moments of the dream, and finish by "being" the dream.

Ann Faraday, an English dream researcher working today, encourages the use of a dream diary to record dreams, and uses the Gestalt technique to find out more about the characters in a dream.

DREAM GROUPS

Described as containing a blend of psychology, mysticism and poetry, a dream group consists of a number of individuals meeting together on a regular basis for the purpose of sharing and working with their dreams. Members of the group can offer their insights and suggestions for how to work with a dream, but are not encouraged to attempt to actually interpret anyone else's. Besides fostering a degree of self-awareness, dream groups allow people to relate to each other at a deeper level than usually occurs in most social interactions. Some groups work with a professional therapist, while others do not find this necessary.

Dream groups are becoming more popular and widespread in the US, but it is also possible to find them in other parts of the world. If such a facility does not exist in your area, it is possible for a group of like-minded people to set up their own group.

SPIRITUAL GROWTH

It is not necessary to have a religious belief to approach dreams from a spiritual perspective. Many people believe that there is more to us than physical form and see dreams as a way of connecting with that mysterious yet crucial part of the self that is often referred to as "spirit". From this perspective dreams become a tool for increased self-knowledge and personal development.

L.M. Savary developed a complex approach to dream interpretation from a Judaeo-Christian perspective, and some of his techniques can be used as a method in themselves. A useful one is the TTAQ (title, theme, affect, question) method. First give your dream a title, next identify the major theme of the dream, and consider how this affected you, noticing for instance any thoughts or feelings that it evoked. Finally explore the question that the dream is trying to help you become aware of.

ABOVE Even if we don't have any religious beliefs it isn't difficult to read a spiritual meaning into our dreams. A particular dream may be full of prosaic, everyday images, but they still have a spiritual significance for the dreamer.

In this dream ... for a timeless moment, I danced, flashed and roared with the storm and seemed to merge with the 'being' at the centre of it.

DR ANN FARADAY

DREAMS AND PREMONITIONS

TALES OF PROPHECY AND FORESEEING THE FUTURE ARE AS OLD AND DIVERSE AS HUMANITY ITSELF. WHILE ORTHODOX
SCIENCE INSISTS THAT PSYCHIC PHENOMENA DO NOT EXIST, DREAMS CONTAINING INFORMATION FROM OTHER PEOPLE OR
NEWS FROM THE FUTURE AS WELL AS DREAMS OF PROPHECY AND WARNING HAVE ALL BEEN RECORDED AT VARIOUS TIMES.
SIMILARLY THERE HAVE BEEN MANY INSTANCES OF DREAMS BEING USED AS A DIAGNOSTIC TOOL FOR HEALING PURPOSES.
HOWEVER WE ACCOUNT FOR SUCH PHENOMENA, THERE IS A BODY OF EXPERIENCE WHICH CANNOT SIMPLY BE DISCOUNTED
OR READILY BE ABSORBED BY OUR RATIONAL, SCIENTIFIC WORLD VIEW.

PRECOGNITIVE DREAMS

An estimated 40 per cent of reported psychic
experiences concern knowing the future in some
way, with dreams being the most common way for
premonitions (precognitions) to appear. Precognitive
dreams are ones where the dreamer somehow
receives information about the future which
subsequently turns out to be verified by events. This
information could not have been obtained or
inferred by any other means.

Traditional societies typically take precognitive
dreams seriously, believing that they may contain
information that could be vital to the survival and
wellbeing of the community. In modern society,
many precognitive dreams have been linked with
major disasters, including the sinking of the *Titanic*

BELOW Are we to take
notice of precognitive
dreams? There have been
cases where the veracity
of such dreams is utterly
convincing to the
dreamer, but does that
mean it is really possible
to dream the future?

in 1912 and the Japanese attack on Pearl Harbor in
1941. Dreams of earthquakes, volcanic eruptions,
and transport disasters on land, sea and air, as well
as the assassinations of public figures have all been
foretold in dreams. There are also instances of
particularly gifted dreamers using knowledge
gleaned in their dreams or in a dream-like state to
help the police solve crimes.

Significant historical figures have also dreamt of
their own destiny. For instance, Genghis Khan,
Oliver Cromwell, Napoleon Bonaparte and Adolf
Hitler all had prophetic dreams of their success in
battle, while the US president Abraham Lincoln saw
his dead body laid out in a coffin two weeks before
he was assassinated. Although Lincoln took the
dream seriously he was unable to avoid its
fulfilment. On a lighter note, there are also many
instances of people dreaming racehorse winners or
lottery numbers, sometimes on a sufficiently regular
basis to make money from it.

THE SLEEPING PROPHET

Perhaps one of the most spectacular revelatory
dreamers of recent times was Edgar Cayce (1877-
1945). Known as the "sleeping prophet", Cayce was
able to diagnose illness, prescribe treatments, and
correctly describe people he had never seen while in
a sleep or trance-like state.

Cayce practised clairvoyance for 43 years and by
the time he died, he had gathered together around
30,000 diagnostic reports and case studies
containing testimonies from his patients and
doctors that vouched for the accuracy of his
diagnosis and treatments. Cayce also used his
psychic abilities to help the police identify and track
down criminals.

Dreams must be heeded and accepted, for a great many of them come true.   PARACELSUS

OTHER TYPES OF PSYCHIC DREAMS

These are also relatively common types of psychic dream phenomena.

dreams of apparitions These dreams involve the deceased, whether you know the person or not. The theory suggests that the person appears in the dream in order to convey a personal message. This message is not necessarily for the dreamer. For instance, it is common for apparitions to appear to people who didn't know them very well, giving them a message to pass on to the loved ones of the deceased.

clairaudient dreams These dreams involve sounds in which you can clearly hear information.

empathic dreams These dreams involve clear and sympathetic feelings or sensations about an event that is occurring as you dream it.

clairvoyant dreams Events occur at the same time as a dream experience of the same event. There is absolutely nothing you can do about changing or preventing anything you see in a clairvoyant dream, although the information can be used to help people.

telepathic dreams Communication is made directly from one energy source to another without any mechanical assistance of any kind. These dreams tend to show us people and events not in our immediate environment. Such dreams sometimes occur when someone is either in danger or in an unusual predicament.

SCIENTIFIC RESEARCH

The problem with premonitions is that the knowledge of the event appears to precede the cause, which in conventional science is impossible. It also raises the principle of free will. Arguments are put forward that the events could be inferred, that the dream was not specific enough, or that they are just coincidences. However research suggests that there is some evidence for foreknowledge. Tests have been conducted where participants guess which card will be shown next, or which light on a panel will come on next, and correct predictions happened surprisingly often.

RIGHT Perhaps dreams are a way for our subconscious to experiment with our hidden fears, rather than any kind of premonition of oncoming disaster that might be creeping up behind us.

NIGHT TRAVELLERS

THE QUESTION ABOUT WHAT HAPPENS TO US WHEN WE ARE ASLEEP IS ONE THAT CONTINUES TO PUZZLE US. SCIENTISTS ARE NOW ABLE TO EXPLAIN THE PHYSIOLOGICAL CHANGES THAT TAKE PLACE IN THE BODY AND ALSO TO MONITOR BRAIN WAVE PATTERNS TO INDICATE STAGES OF SLEEP. PSYCHOLOGISTS CAN EXPLAIN SLEEP AND DREAMING IN TERMS OF UNCONSCIOUS PROCESSES AND RECOGNIZE ARCHETYPAL DREAM SYMBOLS AND PATTERNS. YET NEITHER SCIENCE NOR PSYCHOLOGY CAN ACCOUNT FOR OUT-OF-BODY EXPERIENCES (OBE), WHERE A DREAMER LEAVES THEIR PHYSICAL BODY YET STILL RETAINS CONSCIOUS AWARENESS.

ASTRAL PLANES

Some people believe that dreams are our jumbled and distorted memories of our experiences in the astral kingdom, in which we have wandered while our physical body was sleeping. The astral planes are the supposed non-physical worlds that exist beyond time and space as we know it. Almost all esoteric traditions believe in the astral world in some form or another and that adepts can learn how to "astral travel", or journey into this realm at will.

The astral world is not regarded as an "imaginary" world in contrast to the physical reality of this one, but one that exists in parallel. In fact many spiritual traditions turn the argument on its head, saying that it is our present world that is illusory, and the astral world that is our spiritual home.

BELOW Many cultures believe we leave our body at night and go travelling on the astral plane – in some societies it is the job of the shaman to guide the dreamer and bring them safely back to their body.

THE ASTRAL OR DREAM BODY

In the West, the concept of astral bodies largely originated with Paracelsus, the 16th-century alchemist and healer. Paracelsus was convinced that we are influenced by the sun and moon and planetary constellations, but was not sure how. He came to the conclusion that stellar influences were exerted through what he called the "astral" or invisible energy body that surrounds the physical body. The astral body is roughly the same size and shape as the earthly one, but can detach from it and move about independently.

Psychics who are able to see the astral body maintain that it is connected to the physical body via a "silver cord". When we die, this cord is finally broken and the dream body no longer unites with the physical body.

FLYING DREAMS

During sleep, the astral or dream body lifts away from the physical body to explore other dimensions, but remains connected by the cord. The astral body can travel vast distances, but if the dream body strays too far, the physical body jerks it back again, which may register in sleep as a sense of falling, the sleeper sometimes abruptly waking from the "jolt" with feelings of disorientation and even physical symptoms, such as headaches and nausea. Some commentators believe that dreams of flying are related to psychic out-of-body experiences, the dream body floating weightless into the air, defying the laws of gravity. Such dreams are usually marked by a sense of euphoria and are rarely forgotten by those who have experienced them.

A man dreamt that he slipped out of his flesh just as a snake sheds its old skin. He died the following day. For his soul, which was about to depart from his body, provided him with these images.

ARTEMIDORUS

OUT-OF-BODY EXPERIENCES

The concept of the dream body may help to explain what is happening in an out-of-body experience (OBE). There are many well-documented instances where people have described not being "in" their bodies, but outside them, having no physical sensation but otherwise being able to see and hear what is going on. Some people have reported these experiences at the edge of falling into or out of sleep, describing themselves as "floating" near the ceiling while seeing themselves in bed. There are also many instances where people have reported OBEs while under anaesthesia. As they "float" above their physical body on the operating table, they are able to watch the proceedings and later are able to recount accurate details of what took place.

Many other people have experienced OBEs as a result of a near-death experience or shock. Such experiences are generally life transforming and seem to indicate that we have a level of consciousness that exists independently from our physical condition.

SCIENTIFIC STUDIES

Volunteers who have claimed to be able to generate out-of-body experience at will have been clinically tested. During a reported OBE, EEG readings reveal a change in brain wave patterns from a relaxed alpha rhythm to beta. Beta waves are the ones produced during normal waking activity. Similarly the breathing and heart rate both showed signs of increase, suggesting that some activity or stimulus, similar to a waking condition, was going on in the body. REM was absent, although there were more eye movements than in the usual non-dreaming (orthodox) sleep.

These findings seem to indicate that the sleeping subject was in a relaxed state but with a considerable degree of alertness. They were not, in fact, asleep. Physiological changes and changes in brain wave patterns indicate that something is happening, but more research and validated evidence is needed before science can describe something that "proves" an OBE.

ABOVE Are our dreams a tunnel from this world to the next? Or are our minds perhaps simply experimenting with fears that we avoid when we are awake but still need to confront?

ABOVE LEFT Do dreams give us a little taste of what it is like to be dead? Many claim they do and until it actually happens to us there is no way of being sure.

THE TWILIGHT ZONE

A DREAM IS AN ALTERED STATE OF CONSCIOUSNESS THAT WE FALL INTO DURING SLEEP. HOWEVER THERE ARE OTHER DREAM-LIKE STATES EXPERIENCED WHILE AWAKE OR ON THE BORDERS BETWEEN SLEEP AND WAKING. THESE INCLUDE DAYDREAMS AND HALLUCINATIONS, AS WELL AS HYPNOGOGIC STATES (OCCURRING AT THE EDGE OF SLEEP). ALL ARE CHARACTERIZED BY VIVID IMAGERY AND HEIGHTENED SENSITIVITY. THROUGH TRAINING AND DISCIPLINE, SOME PEOPLE ARE ABLE TO ENTER THESE STATES AT WILL, AND CERTAIN PLANTS AND HERBS HAVE BEEN USED TO ASSIST THE DREAMER'S ENTRY INTO A TRANCE-LIKE STATE. OTHER PEOPLE MAY EXPERIENCE THEM THROUGH MEDITATION.

HYPNOGOGIA

As we relax and drift into sleep, our brain wave pattern lengthens and slows down, changing from beta to alpha, and finally to theta. During this nodding-off stage, we can experience what is known as "hypnogogic" imagery, a series of vivid pictures or surreal imagery that bears little or no relation to waking memories. The imagery doesn't have the narrative quality of most sleeping dreams, but consists of a series of shifting and seemingly unconnected pictures that appear as if from nowhere: an animal, a face or a figure, an eye, a swirling rainbow of colours – the variety is infinite. The same process can also happen in reverse, emerging from sleep into drowsy wakefulness, where the fleeting visions may be referred to as "hypnopompic" imagery. Sometimes these persist into full consciousness when we are fully awake.

This state, also known as hypnogogia, is not only associated with sleep, but may occur in other situations where the brain wave pattern slows down sufficiently and we "switch off", such as during meditation, or even through boredom – as on a long stretch of motorway driving for instance.

HALLUCINATION

The Latin root for the word "hallucination" means "to wander in the mind", while the word "sleep" is derived from the Old English meaning "a vision". While visions, hallucinations and trance-like states are not the same as a sleep-induced dream, they nevertheless represent a dream-like experience where the boundaries between normal waking life and another dimension dissolve and merge. Within these blurred boundaries, there is a fine line between sanity and madness. For instance, people

BELOW As we begin to fall asleep, or sometimes during deep meditation, where the brain slows down, we go through a hypnogogic stage, where our mind tries to make sense of all the images in our head.

> But the dreamers of the day are dangerous people, for they dream their dreams with open eyes and make them come true.
>
> T. E. LAWRENCE

who suffer extreme states of mental illness, or who have misused certain drugs can become overpowered by hallucinations to such an extent that their grip on conventional reality breaks down, and is never really recovered.

SHAMANIC DREAMING

In many traditional cultures, the ability to enter a trance consciously and safely is a skill that is cultivated for the good of the wider community. The role of the dreamer, typically filled by the shaman or priest, is to travel "between the worlds", in search of a vision that can assist or advise his or her people. In fact the word "shaman" may be translated to mean "one who is exalted or lifted up". The shaman has the ability to step outside of their being in ecstatic trance, and is able to enter the dream world at will. While present in the other world they will be able to communicate with the "dream guides" and to bring back gifts of wisdom and healing.

BELOW LEFT Is sleep the same as an hallucination? Research on the brain suggests that the two states are very different although they share similar language, imagery and themes.
BELOW RIGHT The shaman needs to know how to explore the world of the dreamer, and this requires a rigorous and lengthy training.

SACRED HERBS

There are many plants and herbs that are known for their mind-altering effect. Some, such as fly agaric (*Amanita muscaria*) stimulate hallucinations, others such as peyote (*Lophophora williamsii*) produce out-of-body experiences, while cannabis (*C. indica*, *C. sativa*) and morning glory (*Ipomoea*) produce euphoria. Dramatic and vivid dreams can be induced by the infamous opium poppy, shown right, (*Papaver somniferum*). It was while under the influence of opium that Coleridge is alleged to have "visioned" his Kubla Khan poem. In many cultures, including our own, these plant substances have degenerated from their traditional sacred use by initiates in search of higher states of consciousness, into drugs used to escape the realities of everyday life. Most of these drugs are highly addictive and their use is illicit.

To become a shaman involves years of arduous training that typically involves lengthy periods of solitude, fasting and other "tests" designed to build inner strength and preserve sanity in preparation for when the ego's defences are dropped. Certain plants and herbs, as well as incense, talismans and objects of "power", are used to assist the dreamer in entering a trance-like state.

LUCID DREAMING

In 1913, Frederick van Eeden, a Dutch psychiatrist, coined the term "lucid dreams" to describe the state of being aware that you are dreaming, while in the dream state. He based this on his experience of his own numerous lucid dreams. Centuries earlier in ancient Greece, Aristotle had also concluded that during sleep "there is something in consciousness which declares that what then presents itself is but a dream". What happens in the consciousness of the dreamer is something we barely understand, but it seems that lucid dreams introduce us to the part of ourselves that creates our dreams.

ABOVE A lucid dream is one in which we know we are dreaming. They can be very terrifying and unsettling, but if controlled can become liberating and empowering.

DIRECTING A DREAM

Frederick Van Eeden describes a lucid dream he experienced on the night of 9th September 1904. His experience indicates that not only did he retain a level of conscious awareness in the dream, but also that he was able to direct the dream's content and action to some extent.

"I dreamt that I stood at a table before a window. On the table were different objects. I was perfectly aware that I was dreaming and I considered what sorts of experiments I could make ... I took a fine claret glass from the table and struck it with my fist, with all my might, at the same time reflecting how dangerous it would be to do this in waking life; yet the glass remained whole. But lo! When I looked at it again after some time, it was broken. It broke all right, but a little too late, like an actor who misses

ABOVE There will always be clues in a lucid dream that will give the game away and become the trigger that lets us know we are in a dream – minor or major things that are utterly impossible in waking life.

his cue. This gave me a very curious impression of being in a fake world cleverly imitated but with small failures."

SPONTANEOUS LUCIDITY

In general, people who have good recall of their dreams report at least one experience of being in a lucid dream, while for those who regularly record and work with their dreams the experience seems more familiar and frequent. However, we are not really sure what it is that turns a normal dream into a lucid experience. The most common trigger seems to be that the dreamer recognizes a dream-like

RIGHT People like to play around with lucid dreams as it gives us a measure of control – and that means we can direct the dream, face our deepest fears, or live our wildest fantasies in safety.

quality to the events taking place. Sometimes this is when the dreamer becomes aware of a fantastic element, such as a talking dog or being able to fly, while others come to recognize the sensation of the dream state and seem to "just know" they are dreaming. People who record their dreams regularly appear to actually incorporate their recognition of dreaming into the dialogue and action of the dream.

VIRTUAL REALITY

Many people are attracted by the notion of lucid dreams because the idea strikes us as a kind of virtual reality. Once you know that you are in a dream, perhaps you can control the action and influence the course of events – go places, do things, meet people and generally have the kind of experience you want. Because the dream world is not bound by logic or the rules of physics, it is possible to do or be anything that you desire. You can travel through the universe, turn yourself into an alligator, meet a long-lost lover or enjoy an extravagant luxury. This creates an exhilarating sense of freedom and expansion beyond everyday life.

PERSONAL DEVELOPMENT

Many Western therapists regard lucid dreaming as an essential skill on the path to inner development. Charles Tart, an American psychologist, suggests that we use the freedom in lucid dreams to seek or create a wise guide whom we can call upon for advice relating to our spiritual and psychological growth. Lucid dreams can also provide an opportunity to try out new strategies that are different to our habitual responses. By seeing all aspects of the dream as part of yourself, it is possible to stand outside of the role you are playing in the dream, analyse it and change it if you so wish. For instance, instead of fleeing in the face of a tiger, you can try turning around and facing it head on. A recent study indicates that lucid dreamers may have a stronger sense of their individuality and personal power, and may be less likely to succumb to group pressure or conform to society's expectations.

LEARNING TO LUCID DREAM

The most important key to learning how to generate lucid dreams is your level of motivation. The second is being adept at recalling your dreams, something which comes through practice. However, the following techniques may also be used to encourage lucidity:

pre-sleep suggestion As you drift to sleep, repeat a request or statement in your mind about becoming lucid in your dreams.

periodic questioning Develop a "critical-reflective attitude" to your state of consciousness while awake, asking yourself "could I be dreaming now?" at regular intervals throughout the day.

rehearse dreaming Sit down and pretend that you are dreaming. Use your imagination to create a dream.

if this were a dream Several times a day, stop and ask yourself "if this experience were a dream, what would it mean?"

meditation People who regularly practise meditation techniques seem to have more lucid dreams.

dream groups It is possible to join up with other people who are interested in exploring their dreams. People with an established forum in which to discuss their dreams tend to become regular lucid dreamers.

THE SENSE AND SUBSTANCE OF DREAMS

Every night we all dream. What we dream about can be hard to remember, or when we do remember, may be difficult to comprehend. During sleep the brain is active and our dreams are perceived through the deeper layers of the unconscious mind. The unconscious does not communicate in words or through reason, but uses visual images to stimulate intuition and feeling. When we wake we are left with a residual "sense of" something that stays with us through the day, an imprint in our memory like a footstep in the snow.

This section looks at some of the characteristics of dreams, the importance of archetype and symbol, and the logic and landscape of the dreaming world. This information will help you start to make sense of your dreams and of what they are about.

ARCHETYPES

IN ART OR LITERATURE, A RECURRENT SYMBOL OR MOTIF MAY BE DESCRIBED AS AN ARCHETYPE. IN JUNGIAN PSYCHOLOGY IT IS THE TERM USED TO DESCRIBE THE BASIC BUILDING BLOCKS OF THE HUMAN PSYCHE, WHICH RESIDE IN THE COLLECTIVE UNCONSCIOUS. ACCORDING TO JUNG, THE COLLECTIVE UNCONSCIOUS CONTAINS OUR INHERITED CULTURAL, ANCESTRAL AND HISTORIC MEMORIES. THESE ELEMENTS ARE DERIVED FROM THE UNIVERSAL HUMAN EXPERIENCE AND TRANSCEND THE PURELY PERSONAL. ARCHETYPES ARE THE "ORIGINAL PATTERNS", THE DEEPEST PART OF THE HUMAN SOUL THAT FEATURE IN OUR ENDURING FOLKLORE AND ART AND, NOW AND AGAIN, IN OUR DREAMS.

CULTURAL PATTERNS

The collective unconscious may be universal but the form its archetypes take are culture-specific. We see what we have been conditioned to see. For instance in Western culture, angels are celestial beings that mediate between humans and higher powers. In both the Old and New Testaments they appear in dreams and visions, bringing messages from God to the dreamer. Yet in other cultures the concept of the angel is unknown. Among the Sioux Indians of North America it is the full moon that is the heavenly messenger, holding out choices to the dreamer in its hands.

Our dreams therefore are patterned according to our culture, giving us roots deep into our ancestral and historic past. It is these "cultural pattern" or archetypal dreams that seem to be some form of communication from the beyond, from something bigger and outside of our "little selves". They are the ones that wake us up with a start.

DREAMS BIG AND SMALL

Malinowski, a contemporary of Jung's, distinguished between two types of dream. Cultural pattern or archetypal dreams he calls "official" dreams, while "free" dreams are those that are entirely of our own making. Jung refers to these official dreams as the big or meaningful dreams as opposed to the little or everyday dreams. The little dreams are the ones where we seem to be doing our mental filing, sorting and processing all the information we receive while awake. They are the ones where we can easily identify the imagery and symbolism: "Oh, yes, I dreamed of that because I had watched a particular film just before going to bed", or "Ah, I know why I dreamed of that, it was because we were talking about it earlier in the day". The big dreams on the other hand are the ones that seem to mean something profound and defy rational explanation.

From the collective unconscious we draw images (archetypes) of extraordinary potential and power. These images present themselves to us in our big dreams. The big dreams are the ones we remember, that haunt us. They are packed with vivid imagery, symbolism and metaphor that are too powerful to be held in our mental grasp. These images are sometimes disturbing, frequently new and very often wonderful. They seem larger than life and to come from another dimension, and can provoke the question: "Am I dreaming, or being dreamed?"

BELOW No matter what our culture, we do all seem to share certain imagery – or archetypes – that we all respond to in a similar way, even if the meaning behind the image has different shades of interpretation.

We may expect to find in dreams everything that has ever been of significance in the life of humanity.

CARL JUNG

THE POWER OF ARCHETYPES

Examining these archetypes is essential if we are to understand our dreams and the personal messages they hold for us. The archetypes are there to challenge us, to stretch us, to take us out of our normal everyday life and throw us back into the mysterious world of myths and magic. They are there to remind us that we are more than going to work, watching TV or eating out at the latest restaurants. At rock bottom, we are creatures of spirit and imagination, intuition and mystery. No matter how "civilized" we become, like a tidal wave an archetypal dream will suddenly appear, a shocking reminder that we are more than the little selves of our everyday life.

THE TIMING OF BIG DREAMS

Times of change and transition are generally recognized as "stress points". This is because there is a wealth of new material for us to process and integrate into the psyche and our normal ego defences are weakened. This may help to explain why a powerful dream is more likely to get through to us at such times.

Archetypal dreams often occur when we are undergoing major life events. Typical instances include puberty, marriage, pregnancy, death or divorce as well as children leaving home, taking up a new job or moving house. Major events do not have to be personal to trigger an archetypal dream. Dramatic global news can also affect us at a deep soul level and there are typically many reported incidences of big dreams after major world events, such as the unexpected death of a public figure or outbreaks of war and violence.

ABOVE Archetypal dreams often occur when we are going through life's rites of passage – as if they are needed most then.
ABOVE LEFT Most archetypes are instantly recognizable and we would probably associate this character with ancient wisdom and nobility.

LEFT Perhaps your dreams contain images that your mind has taken with it from your day's activities. If you watch television in bed it seems logical that visual elements from that will be revisited in a dream.

JUNGIAN ARCHETYPES

In his investigations into the collective unconscious, Jung formulated several archetypal forces or principles. These may not be definitive, but they nevertheless remain a handy and convenient tool for making sense of our dreams.

THE PERSONA

The conscious personality, the Persona, is akin to Freud's concept of the ego. It is the person we present to the outside world, the mask we wear in order to protect our most real and vulnerable self. To find the Persona in our dreams is to look for a symbolic representation of "me".

We have many guises and wear many masks depending on the social role we are playing. Responsible parent, respected professional and rebellious teenager are just a few examples. Appearing naked in a dream is an indicator that the mask has slipped, our Persona is absent and we are literally naked before others, physically, emotionally and even spiritually. If we feel the mask is tarnished we may appear as a scarecrow, a tramp, or a degenerate. If we feel the mask is too firmly in place we may wear armour or a visor.

THE SHADOW

Jung described the Shadow as a "splinter personality". Anything that does not fit with how we like to see ourselves is pushed into the background, repressed into the unconscious. Yet no matter how hard we try to keep it under control, every now and again it erupts, like a wilful and disobedient child. The Shadow is our dark side, our "sinful" nature that we judge and condemn as wrong and bad. It is our temper tantrums, black moods, anger, violence, lust, greed and unspeakable desires. It is the things we fear and hate the most.

We are very afraid of the Shadow, for it has the power to rip away the mask and reveal our true face. In our dreams it may appear as a shadowy figure, a cloaked evil-doer, a malignant force threatening to overpower us. Yet Jung did not perceive the Shadow as inherently evil, merely "somewhat inferior, primitive, unadapted and awkward". It does things in the old way, as Jung put it, and its messages are often actually for our own good.

THE ANIMA AND ANIMUS

We each wear the mask of our gender. Yet within every man and woman resides the seed of the opposite sex. "Anima" and "Animus" were the terms coined by Jung to personify the "inner woman" and the "inner man", or the feminine part of a man's personality and the masculine part of a woman's.

Both the Anima and Animus are shaped by the child's experience of his or her mother and father. Broadly speaking however, the Animus is the hero within, practical, adventurous, independent and self-assured. The Anima is the heroine, both goddess and seductress. She is sensitive, compassionate, sensual and instinctive. It must be remembered that these are psychological attributes rather than characteristics of men and women as such. When these qualities are not integrated into the psyche, we project them on to other people, particularly our partners, in our desire for that perfect person who, we believe, will make our dreams come true.

THE TRICKSTER

Hard to define because he is always one step ahead, the Trickster leads us a merry dance as we follow pipe dreams. He is the shape shifter, the joker in the pack and the jester or clown. His is the leering, jeering face in the carnival, painted and seductive. He is the Pied Piper, the Lord of the Dance who offers us delight and pleasure, but if we follow his call we will end up a laughing stock, with dust in our mouths.

Although a mischievous fraudster and saboteur, the Trickster's antics can also be corrective. With great skill he pricks the balloon of our inflated sense of self, mocking our vanities and self-obsessions, ridiculing our ambitions and desires. Not of this world, the Trickster is also the shaman, the one who can enter the realm of magic and interpret our dreams. He represents our intuitive side.

THE DIVINE CHILD

A symbol of innocence and purity, the Divine Child embodies birth and growth, potential and latent energy. The Divine Child is a link between past, present and future, a mediator who brings healing and wholeness, and possesses enormous transforming power. Symbols for the Divine Child include the changeling, the jewel, the flower and the chalice. By becoming the Divine Child ourselves we strip away all our preconceptions and judgements, as well as our ideas and goals. The Divine Child is a return to innocence, a readiness to be reborn without the mask.

THE LITTLE PRINCE

The following extract is from Antoine de Saint-Exupéry's novel *The Little Prince* in which he describes a dream-like landscape and an archetypal Divine Child figure.

"Look very carefully at the landscape so as to be sure to recognize it ... And if you should happen to come upon this spot, please do not hurry on. Wait a little, exactly under the star. Then, if a child comes towards you, if he laughs, if he has golden locks and if he refuses to answer questions, you will surely guess who he is."

ABOVE The image of the Divine Child is a very powerful one and it has inspired painters and poets for centuries. Here it is contrasted with the archetype of the hero, the youthful aspect of the Father.

LEFT The image of the Divine Child combined with that of the Great Mother is so powerful that it has inspired religions that have affected millions and filled them with awe.

THE GREAT MOTHER

From the Great Mother's loins springs all of humanity, created and birthed from her womb and her fruitfulness. This archetype has three aspects: virgin, mother and crone, each of these having a positive and a negative face. The virgin is a young bare-breasted girl garlanded with spring flowers. She dances, sings, and plays music, she is a creature of the meadows and fields. In her negative aspect she is a seductress, purposely attracting and then spurning her suitors. The round-bellied "earth" mother is the healer and nurturer, caring for the physical and emotional needs of her family. She inhabits the kitchen and bake house, the summer lodges, the woods and the glades. Or else she is the "terrible mother", possessive, demanding and devouring. The crone is the wise woman and priestess. She is intuitive and free thinking, living life according to her own rules. She possesses psychic, magical powers. Her other side is the ugly hag, a nightmare creature of the forests and caves, the underground, the underworlds. She is the evil sorceress and harpy.

THE GREAT FATHER

Parallel to the Great Mother is the Great Father. His aspects complement those of the Mother: prince, father and hermit, each with a positive and a negative side. The prince is the young man with high ideals, setting out on the quest of life. He is the dreamer and poet and is capable of greatness. In his negative aspect he is a vagabond and wastrel, the lazy lout who thinks the world owes him a living. He uses women to gratify his sexual desires.

The father is the hunter and provider. He procreates and preserves the race and represents standards and ideals to live up to. He is an authority figure and we seek his approval, but his judgements are fair. On the negative side he is the despot and ogre, an authoritarian figure who is sadistic and uncaring. The hermit excludes himself from society to nurture his soul in prayer and meditation. He is the "wise ancient", the guru, priest and spirit guide, who can help us find our inner light. He brings

---

FINDING YOUR ARCHETYPES

Some archetypes will have more meaning for you than others. These are the ones most likely to appear in your dreams. Draw up a list of archetypes that have the most meaning for you. This could contain characters and personalities, as well as objects and situations. Use the list to help you, adding or deleting any as appropriate.

archetypal characters

king/queen	alchemist	mythical beast	traveller
prince/princess	artist	(sphinx, unicorn,	skeleton
baby/child	monk/nun	dragon)	criminal
messenger	priest/priestess	jester	prisoner
angel	any animal	pregnant woman	ghost
devil	crows/other birds	lovers	

archetypal objects and locations

sun	rainbow	graveyard	chalice
moon	temple/church	landscape	jewels or money
stars	battlefield	sailing boat	
the four elements	clouds	cave	
lightning	maze	sword	

practical understanding to our problems and dilemmas and a sense of personal power. In his dark aspect he is the black magician who misuses his powers for personal gain.

OTHER ARCHETYPES

Archetypal themes and patterns can also appear in many other forms. For instance the journey, the eternal triangle, temptation and redemption, birth, death and disaster are all common themes that appear in myth and religion as well as in our dreams. The four elements (fire, water, earth and air) are archetypal energies, representing the natural forces of the universe that shape and sustain our lives. Animals too can be archetypal symbols. For instance, a dog may characterize loyalty, a hawk clear vision and a cat freedom and independence. Esoteric arts, such as astrology and the tarot, as well as the world's greatest myths are also based on archetypal symbols, which may help to explain their enduring fascination. Defying rational explanation they strike a chord deep within us, speaking the eternal language of the soul.

UNDERSTANDING ARCHETYPES

Archetypes permeate every facet of our lives. To begin to understand how they work and how they relate to your life, try the following questionnaire for fun. Don't think about the answers but go for the one that first comes to mind, elaborating on it as much as possible. You might be surprised at the results!

1 Choose a flower to represent yourself. What does it say about you that is hard to express in words alone?

2 What is your favourite colour and why do you like it?

3 Which is your favourite domestic animal? What qualities does it have that resonate with you?

4 Describe your favourite foods. How do you feel when you eat these foods?

5 What is your favourite tree? What is it about the tree that you especially like?

6 What kind of water do you like best: rivers, streams, lakes or the sea? Do you know what this kind of water says to you?

7 If you could shape shift, which animal would you like to become? Can you say what it is about this animal that you find so inspiring?

explanation

1 The flower represents your attitude to your soul.

2 The colour represents your emotional attitude.

3 The domestic animal represents the qualities you look for in your friends.

4 The food represents how you feel about your body and sex as a physical activity.

5 The tree represents your attitude towards life in general.

6 The water you have chosen represents your sexuality.

7 The wild animal represents the hidden you beneath the mask.

FAR LEFT AND LEFT
Archetypes help us understand ourselves and our partners, friends and family. By identifying different archetypes, such as the hero (far left) and the unicorn (left) and how they affect us, we can learn a lot about ourselves.

LEVELS OF DREAMING

THE UNCONSCIOUS IS MADE UP OF DIFFERENT LAYERS, REPRESENTING SUCCESSIVELY DEEPER STRATA OF THE MIND. FREUD CONCEPTUALIZED THESE LAYERS AT TWO LEVELS: THE PRECONSCIOUS AND THE PERSONAL UNCONSCIOUS. TO THESE JUNG ADDED A THIRD LEVEL, WHICH HE REFERRED TO AS THE COLLECTIVE UNCONSCIOUS. THERE MAY ALSO BE A DIMENSION OF THE MIND THAT CAN PRODUCE VISION-LIKE DREAMS OF EXTRAORDINARY POWER AND SIGNIFICANCE. OUR DREAMS ARISE FROM THESE DIFFERENT LEVELS, AND ALTHOUGH ANY DREAM CAN CONTAIN MATERIAL FROM MORE THAN ONE LEVEL, USUALLY ONE OR OTHER LEVEL PREDOMINATES.

BELOW Level one dreams are most often associated with the preconscious; the most accessible part of our mind. The elements within these dreams may be random mental images with no meaning.

LEVEL ONE DREAMS

These dreams are associated with the preconscious, the most accessible part of the mind. Level one dreams contain material that can be easily linked to waking life. These dreams tend to revolve around the events of the day, and opinion is divided as to whether or not they are particularly meaningful.

Some would say that these dreams represent random, jumbled nonsense. They are a way of the mind unburdening itself and have no particular significance. Others suggest that trivial events should not necessarily be automatically dismissed: they may be used as a "way in" to deeper levels of the mind which are more difficult to access directly.

LEVEL TWO DREAMS

Dreams at this level are capable of giving us insights which we could not achieve during normal waking life. These dreams, from the personal unconscious, can include forgotten memories, repressed wishes and fears, and unacknowledged emotions and expectations. The symbolism of these dreams is uniquely personal to the dreamer and the dream scenario is usually quite different to anything in waking life. Such dreams usually have an intriguing quality to them and are not easily forgotten.

LEVEL THREE DREAMS

The collective unconscious is a storehouse of archetypal themes and symbols, forming the raw material for the deepest longings and aspirations of the human race. This level transcends the purely personal. Dreams from this level are concerned with profound issues such as life and death, love, transformation and spirituality. Dreams in this category are much less common, although people engaged in self-exploration practices such as psychotherapy or meditation, or who consciously choose to work with their dreams in some way, often report an increase in level three dreams.

COSMIC DREAMS

On very rare occasions, maybe once in a lifetime only, you may encounter an extremely important and extraordinary dream that is truly awe-inspiring. Cosmic dreams go even further than level-three type

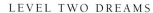

Sometimes dreams alter the course of an entire life.

JUDITH DUERK

dreams. They are ones in which the qualities of the universe itself are the major themes. They are made up of formless shapes and colours, a swirling mass of light and dark and shade with no recognizable objects or identifiable substance. Cosmic dreams are an attempt by the unconscious to make sense of the vastness of the universe and our place within it. The Moscow-born writer and mystic, P.D. Ouspensky (1878-1947) said such dreams "disclose to us the mysteries of being, show the governing laws of life, and bring us into contact with higher forces". These dreams have the capacity to change our life.

THE TUNNEL OF LIGHT

A man had the following cosmic dream when he was 41 years old, and finds that it has stayed with him through the following years:

I was rushing down this incredible tunnel of light – but it was a dark light. I had no body and was pure spirit, pure energy. There was a sound, a voice which was saying something like, "You are entering sector 16". At the end of the tunnel I came to a sudden stop and was aware that I had arrived at a sort of hole in a cliff face, but this was a cliff face a million miles high. The hole was halfway up and I was looking out over a wide plain that was completely occupied by some divine being. It was a sort of giant eye but there wasn't a physical eye – only a divine way of seeing everything. As I stood there I was aware that this eye was turning towards me, was going to look at me. I felt I wasn't worthy. This wasn't my time. I was frightened and was immediately whisked back up the tunnel. I woke up sweating and very shaken.

I have thought about this dream almost every day since having it seventeen years ago. I am determined to be "worthy" next time I go back. I think the next time will be when I die. I believe that what I was given a glimpse of was my own mortality, my own death. This dream has had a huge impact on me. Everything I do is judged against that worthiness. I can't explain what it is that would make something I do worthy, but I just know instinctively what is right and wrong."

ABOVE Each of the images in our dreams has been carefully chosen so that it means something to us, the dreamer.

LEFT Into our dream worlds we take with us the images we have accumulated through our lives.

DREAM LOGIC

LOGIC IS NOT THE FORTE OF THE DREAMING MIND. IN OUR DREAMS THE IMPOSSIBLE BECOMES POSSIBLE AND THE NONSENSICAL APPEARS PERFECTLY NORMAL, AS PEOPLE, ANIMALS, OBJECTS AND PLACES BEHAVE IN BIZARRE AND UNACCOUNTABLE WAYS. FREUD ONCE REMARKED THAT ANYONE WHO BEHAVED WHILE AWAKE AS THEY DO IN THEIR DREAMS WOULD BE REGARDED AS INSANE. IN THE WORLD OF DREAMS, THE NORMAL RULES OF LOGIC, REASON AND "COMMON SENSE" ARE THROWN TO THE WINDS AS EVENTS APPEAR TO KALEIDOSCOPE INTO A THEATRE OF THE ABSURD. YET STRANGE THOUGH IT MAY SEEM, OUR DREAMS DO IN FACT HAVE A CURIOUS LOGIC OF THEIR OWN.

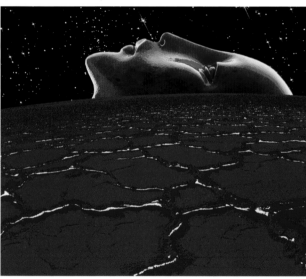

ABOVE All our dreams have their own curious dream logic, stemming from our own personal logic. Once we crack the code all our dreams can be understood.
ABOVE RIGHT It is useful to look at other people's dream logic but bear in mind they might only match yours slightly, more likely they will bear no resemblance at all.

FREUD'S DREAM LOGIC

Intrigued by the absurdity of dreams, Freud began his investigation into how dreams work. His work claims that dreams express an element of logical connection in four different ways: simultaneity, contiguity, transformation and similarity.

When two elements in a dream are presented close together, simultaneity suggests that an intimate relationship exists between the two. Dream combinations are not randomly formed but have meaning within the dream. Contiguity is when dream elements occur sequentially, and transformation is when one thing turns into another. Similarity is the direct or indirect association between things in the dream.

The work of American psychologists Hall and Nordby adds the idea of "relative consistency" to Freud's ideas, noticing that dream motifs have a certain frequency and uniformity about them.

YOUR DREAM LOGIC

Other people's ideas may be helpful when practising dream interpretation, but they will not necessarily fit with everyone's dreams all of the time. We all have our own unique dream logic which may be completely different from anyone else's. If you are keeping a dream record, see if you can find a consistency of pattern to your dreams. It may be that you always appear as yourself or always as someone else. Your dream logic is a bit like Woody Allen films. You may see a different film each time but the style is consistent and recognizable. You get to know your way round as you study the subject.

MICE AND SPIDERS

Your unique dream logic invariably extends to your dream symbolism and will most likely influence the type of archetypes you are working with. These represent what you need to "bring to the surface"

What is life? An illusion, a shadow, a story. And the greatest good is little enough: for all life is a dream and dreams themselves are only dreams.
PEDRO CALDERON DE LA BARCA

emotionally and indicate the sort of imagery you feel more or less comfortable with. For even in the depths of the most awful nightmare, you will find yourself being terrorized by the sort of thing that you already know you find scary. In a sense this is a comforting thought, because you will not frighten yourself in your dreams with an image that is totally alien. If it is mice and spiders that scare you in waking life, then they are the most likely creatures to pop up and scare you in your dreams. Conversely if it is the Bogey Man, ghosts or monsters that terrify you, then that is what will stalk the nightmare corridors of your dreaming mind.

BLOOD IN THE TAPS

Your own curious dream logic is likely to remain fairly constant over the years and you will gradually come to know your dreams, and yourself, pretty well. Once you know your own dream logic you can to a certain extent ignore what is following those predictable patterns. For instance, if someone dreams that water comes out of the taps, then their logic is following a natural course. If, however, they

ABOVE Whatever scares or disturbs you in your waking life is likely to scare you just as much in your dreams. The nightmares that frighten you will carry images that you have an instant fearful reaction to.

always dream that blood comes out of the taps then that is their unique dream logic. Neither dream is good or bad, right or wrong. They are merely the unique expressions of two different dreamers whose minds are processing their unconscious material while they are asleep.

DREAMS AND EVERYDAY LIFE

There does seem to be a close relationship between what happens in our "real" lives and what happens in our dreams. The situations may change but the rules governing them tend to be the same as in everyday life. For instance if you are always concerned with what people wear, then it is likely that clothes and the way they are worn will be just as important in your dreams. If, on the other hand, you are more interested in what people say, then it is likely your dreams will follow a similar pattern.

DREAM SCENERY

DREAMS HAVE TO BE SET SOMEWHERE, TO HAVE A PHYSICAL SITUATION THAT THEY TAKE PLACE IN. THIS IS THE DREAM SCENERY, SIMILAR TO THE BACKDROP OF A THEATRE STAGE. THE LOCATION AND PROPS PROVIDE A CONTEXT FOR THE DREAM AND GIVE CLUES ABOUT THE ACTION THAT IS TAKING PLACE. FOR MOST OF US MOST OF THE TIME, THE CHARACTERISTICS OF THIS BACKDROP REMAIN MUCH THE SAME AS IN EVERYDAY LIFE. IT IS UNUSUAL FOR DREAMS TO BE SET IN A LANDSCAPE WHERE, FOR EXAMPLE, EVERYTHING IS PERMANENTLY UPSIDE DOWN. IT IS MUCH MORE LIKELY THAT THE SCENERY WILL BE THE RIGHT WAY UP AND THE DREAM ACTORS AND PROPS BEHAVE ACCORDING TO THE NATURAL LAWS OF PHYSICS.

BELOW RIGHT Once we are immersed in the dream the landscape will appear real; it is only when we wake that it seems odd. It may be a symbolic or real place, or even both.
BELOW Interpreting the landscapes in your dreams will depend on what significance they have to you in real life. Tall buildings would have suggested the phallus to Freud, but to you they might represent anything from soaring ambition to intimidation.

SURREAL LANDSCAPES

Now and again of course, dream settings and characters do not obey natural laws. Trees may appear upside down, the sky may be green, the sea a brilliant shade of yellow, cats may swim and people may fly weightless above the ground. Within the context of the dream, all of these things appear perfectly normal. It is only when we wake that they strike us as odd, as the rational mind tries to make sense of the illogical and therefore impossible.

These surreal dreams are often the ones that stick in the memory and usually have particular significance for the dreamer. The landscape is what we would focus on when trying to interpret the dream, although the conclusions we reach will depend on each individual.

According to Freud, the landscape of our dreams can be interpreted, and represents the uncharted territory of the unconscious mind and our repressed sexual longings.

> Then suddenly I ... fly slowly over the lane, over the houses, and then over the Golden Horn in the direction of Stamboul. I smell the sea, feel the wind, the warm sun. This flying gives me a wonderfully pleasant sensation... P. D. OUSPENSKY

INTERPRETING THE LANDSCAPE

In a Freudian world, soft round or curvy shapes and narrow indentations represent the female form. For instance, hills represent a woman's breasts, belly or womb, and a dark doorway or passageway, her vagina. Alternatively, hard, upright or elongated shapes represent the male form. Mountain peaks, tall buildings, a train and an aeroplane are all phallic symbols. Only you can decide if these ideas have meaning for you in the context of your dreams.

Jung did not interpret the dream landscape in the same way as Freud, yet he nevertheless believed that the place where the dream is staged makes a tremendous difference to the way the dream is interpreted. A dream that is set in a wood or forest has quite a different feel about it to one that is set in a living room or office. Some dream experts believe that dreams staged in a man-made setting are more based on the concerns of the personality, while those dreams that are set in nature come from the deeper reaches of the soul.

MOODS AND FEELINGS

It is not only the physical nature of the dream setting that is important, but the mood or atmosphere it inspires. The dream landscape has the power to provoke feelings and emotions in the dreamer. Although the scenery may look the same as it does in ordinary life, it may take on a curious surreal quality, appearing melting and hypnotic, as deeply experienced and more real than real. People in a state of hallucination have reported similar occurrences, experiencing a world where walls are sad or happy, trees can sing and dance, and crockery can throw itself at you in a fit of angry pique.

Yet dream scenery does not need to take on a life of its own for it to inspire mood and feelings. Some of the most lasting impressions of our dreams

LEFT Dream landscape not only refers to natural scenery, but to any context in which your dream takes place, inside or out. You might dream about your own living room – it would still be your dream landscape.

COMMON DREAM SETTINGS

Research indicates that the most frequent dream setting is a building, usually a domestic residence, with the living room, bedroom or kitchen being the most common place. The average number of characters in a dream is three, with strangers appearing slightly more often than friends or family members. Predominant dream activities are action-based, such as walking or running, followed by talking, sitting, socializing and playing. The most common emotions are apprehension and anger, followed by happiness and excitement.

are fragments of a landscape dimly remembered. Beautiful, awe-inspiring, tantalizing or downright peculiar, the dream setting is not only a backdrop for the action to take place, but is an integral part of the dream's content and the message it is trying to convey to the dreamer.

BELOW The dream setting allows us the freedom to imagine that anything can take place; that anything is possible, it doesn't have to be real or feasible, and it is important to examine why you have dreamt it like this.

NIGHTMARES

Almost everyone knows what it's like to have a nightmare. The Chinese describe them as dreams of terror and dread, with the power to jolt us out of sleep. Witnessing acts of horror or being in some kind of danger are the most frequent nightmare scenarios. These are usually accompanied by feelings of helplessness and paralysis, of being lost or out of control and at the mercy of an external agent or event. For those who suffer from frequent nightmares going to bed is filled with fear. Sleep is not renewing and refreshing, but is more like going into a stressful situation, night after night.

THE SUBJECTIVITY OF NIGHTMARES

Although we share a broad consensus about what is frightening, the content of our nightmares is always subjective. What is frightening in one person's dream world may seem innocuous in someone else's. What makes a nightmare upsetting is how it feels, the emotional experience, rather than the symbols or events in themselves. Consequently people who are emotionally sensitive seem to be more likely to experience nightmares than those who can shrug unwanted thoughts and feelings away. This may help explain why people with a creative bent, as well as young children, seem to suffer more frequent nightmares than other people.

WHY WE HAVE NIGHTMARES

Although nightmares are unpleasant, they may have a positive intention. They can be a message from the unconscious mind, a way of alerting us to something that is going on in our waking life that we need to become more aware of. When this is the case, the nightmare may recur, growing progressively more frightening until we understand what it is about and can root out the cause. Sometimes nightmares may be signs of illness and/or drug reactions, so do check with your doctor to eliminate this possibility.

CREATIVE VISUALIZATION

When nightmares become a real problem, and begin to disturb your waking life too, there are self-help measures you can take to reduce their frequency and intensity. The following suggestions are based on the techniques of creative visualization. Use them to begin to learn how to tap into the powers of your imagination in order to create change.

LEFT The more sensitive we are, the more artistic and creative, the more likely it is we are going to have nightmares. If you suffer from them, you might take some comfort from that fact.

To sleep: perchance to dream: ay, there's the rub:
For in that sleep of death what dreams may come...

WILLIAM SHAKESPEARE, HAMLET

CREATING AN IMAGINARY SCENE

Some people are able to visualize very easily; for others it might take some practice. You are trying to develop your ability to experience a mental escape from the scenes of your nightmares. Aim to make your imaginary scene such a strong image in your mind that it travels with you into your dream, and becomes your refuge over which you have control.

1 Sit in a quiet place where you feel safe and won't be disturbed. Close your eyes, breathe gently and allow yourself to relax.

2 Now imagine yourself in a beautiful place. This may be outside in nature, or indoors. It can be a real or an imaginary place. Visualize the scene as fully as possible, noticing the objects or scenery that surround you, any sounds or smells, whether it is warm or cool. Notice how you feel and what you are wearing. If you find yourself stopping at various points as you go through your imaginary scene, take notice of where you stop and then start again. It may take a few stops and starts to develop the scene in your mind's eye, but with time and regular practice it will come.

3 When you are comfortable with your scene, experiment by making small changes in it. For instance, you could change the colour of the walls, or add an animal that you like, or maybe a doorway or pathway. Continue to practise until you feel confident that the power of your own imagination has been added to your collection of skills. If at any time you start experiencing a negative reaction to what you are imagining, stop the scene and start again.

WORKING WITH NIGHTMARES

When you are able to create an imaginary scene and play about with it at will you are ready to use the technique with your nightmares. For some people, nightmares arise as a result of an actual trauma. Traumatic events can be too much for us to deal with at the time, so for the sake of preserving our sanity, they get pushed into the basement of the unconscious. Later the unexplored material may resurface in our dreams, perhaps so that any leftover memories and feelings associated with the event can be worked through and healed in relative safety. You may need to seek professional help when dealing with these sorts of nightmares.

1 Write down a recent nightmare. After you have written it down, allow yourself to change the nightmare in any way you wish, writing out a new and less threatening scenario.

2 Using your creative imagination, visualize the new dream you have written. See the scene in as much detail as possible. Let it play through your mind for 5-10 minutes, as if it is a new dream that you are actually experiencing.

3 Imagine this new dream at least once a day for a week, preferably before going to sleep. It is best to work with one dream at a time and not more than three a week.

After three months you should see some improvement in your nightmares. If no change is happening, change the dream again, creating a different scenario.

ABOVE The beautiful imaginary place that you create in your mind can take many forms. If you always return to the same place it can become more and more real, with a potency that can overcome the nightmare.

CHILDREN AND DREAMS

WE ARE BORN WITH THE CAPACITY TO DREAM. EVEN IN THE WOMB INDICATORS OF THE DREAMING STATE ARE PRESENT AND DREAMS PLAY AN IMPORTANT ROLE IN THE LIFE OF THE GROWING CHILD. THE JOURNEY OF CHILDHOOD IS THE GROWTH AND DEVELOPMENT OF INNATE CAPACITIES AS THE YOUNG PERSON LEARNS ABOUT THEMSELVES AND THE WORLD THEY LIVE IN. GROWING UP IS THE JOURNEY FROM AN INSTINCTUAL, UNCONSCIOUS STATE TO CONSCIOUS SELF-AWARENESS. CHILDREN'S DREAMS HAVE AN IMPORTANT PART TO PLAY IN THIS PROCESS. THEY ARE ONE OF THE WAYS THAT CHILDREN EXPRESS THEIR EMERGING IDENTITY AND INDICATE THEIR STATE OF MIND.

MYSTERY AND IMAGINATION

By the time we reach adulthood, we have reached some understanding about how the world is put together and our place in it. We approach the world with reason and have a sense of self or identity. For the developing child, things are not so clearly defined. The world is a place of mystery and fascination and the boundaries between fantasy and reality are blurred. It can be hard to tell where dreams end and imagination takes over. Talk to children about what happens in their dreams and

BELOW Children can be paralysed by the most intense nightmares and can be afraid to go to sleep. But without any fears children sleep with such serenity it often seems they are undisturbed by any kind of dream at all.

they will tell you of noble adventure stories where they play the hero and save the world, or else they'll tell you scary tales of monsters and demons and frightening fantasies. They also act out these fantasies in their play, both alone and when they are with other children.

Although young children may not understand their thoughts and feelings, they experience them with a rawness and intensity that as adults we may find hard to comprehend. The experience of children's daily life is much closer to the world of dreams. Children's dreams are vivid, intense and frequent. Appealing to their sense of mystery and imagination, every night they journey into a magical world of the unexpected and unexplained.

DREAM CONTENT

As we would expect, children's dreams reflect their waking lives and preoccupations. For instance, a young boy experiencing sibling rivalry may dream of quite happily killing his baby sister. To a parent, such a dream may appear alarming and shocking, but it does not mean the boy really wants to commit such an act, but is expressing his feelings of jealous outrage towards his rival, without any kind of moral inhibitions, in the dream. It is not surprising that parents and family members, rather than strangers, figure largely in children's dreams, as these are the people that fill up their waking lives. Friends and acquaintances tend to play an important role in the dreams of later childhood. Animals also feature strongly in children's dreams in various ways. Dreams tend to become longer and more complex, and more similar to the dreams of adults, as the child gets older.

If you talk to your children, you can help them to keep their lives together. If you talk to them skilfully, you can help them to build future dreams.

JIM ROHN

CHILDREN'S NIGHTMARES

Because children imagine and dream in glorious technicolour, their nightmares will be all the more frightening, all the more real. Similarly although we know there aren't really any bogey men or vampires, or monsters that are going to eat us, children don't have a cast-iron certainty about these things. As parents all we will get is a screaming child. We won't necessarily know what sparked it off, but what we do know is that the child is terrified and upset. In such a state of terror, the child needs to be reassured and to feel the comfort and safety offered by the parent. You can try telling them that if the monster appears again in a dream that it is to go away because you say so. Later you may be able to talk to the child to find out what it was all about.

However, for children to reveal shocking or disturbing dreams to their parents requires a climate of trust and sensitivity. Children won't tell their dreams if they think they will get into trouble, or that their parents will be dismissive. Sometimes children will avoid telling the truth in order to cover up what they feel their dream was really about.

AN OUT-OF-BODY EXPERIENCE

Children's nightmares are often triggered by emotional upsets. For instance, suffering disappointments, being unjustly punished, missing a favourite person, or having problems at school are some fairly common experiences. Although these problems cannot be corrected instantly, you can go a long way towards reassuring the child that they are loved and safe.

The following account is from an adult who recalls making up a dream as a child to satisfy his mother's curiosity, and reassure her. He has never told her what really happened.

"Aged about six I had a powerful experience, perhaps it was astral projection, perhaps not. But I did feel weirdly out of my body, hovering near the ceiling. I was absolutely terrified of this and screamed. My mother came rushing upstairs full of concern, but I didn't know what to tell her, it was so out of my experience, so I opted for lying. I told her that there had been a man in my room with a knife and he was going to kill me, going to kill all of us. My mother comforted me and dried my tears. For years afterwards, she talked about this 'nightmare' of mine. She told all my relatives and I never once corrected her. Even when I was grown up, I never had the heart to tell her that the content of my nightmare wasn't true, and I'd had a frightening out-of-body experience. I didn't tell her because I thought she wouldn't believe me or think it silly."

BELOW LEFT Your child may not understand or be able to articulate what they are dreaming about, so pressurizing them to tell you won't work.
BELOW Children, just like adults, are trying to make sense of the waking world in their dreams. Moments of confusion and insecurity will be reflected in their dreams and become part of the process of working out life's scary bits.

Working with Dreams

There are many different kinds of dream. Some are at a relatively superficial level. These are largely concerned with daily trivia and seem to represent a cataloguing of the day's events. Others seem to bubble up from the deepest, darkest corners of the psyche and are not so easily understood. These are the ones that usually strike us as important in some way, even if we cannot be sure why. Learning to capture these "dreams from the deep" and finding ways to decode their meaning is what the following pages are all about.

Keeping a dream diary, working with dream tools and using your dreams for problem-solving as well as learning how to control your dreams are some of the different ways you can work with your dreams. With these keys you will be able to unlock the secrets of your dreams. This will bring a greater understanding of yourself and your relationships and increase your capacity to live life to the full.

UNDERSTANDING DREAMS

THERE ARE PROBABLY HUNDREDS OF WAYS OF INTERPRETING DREAMS – FROM FREUD TO JUNG, FROM MESSAGES FROM THE GODS TO DIVINATION, FROM CHEMICAL REACTIONS TO EMOTIONAL REORDERING. WHETHER WE OPT FOR A PSYCHOLOGICAL, SPIRITUAL OR SCIENTIFIC PERSPECTIVE HOWEVER, ALL OUR DREAMS STEM FROM THE DREAMER. IN YOUR DREAMS, THE IMAGERY WILL CHANGE, THE SITUATIONS AND CIRCUMSTANCES WILL CHANGE AND THE CAUSES OF THE DREAMS WILL CHANGE. THE ONLY COMMON DENOMINATOR, THE ONLY CONSTANT, IS YOU. IN WORKING OUT WHAT YOUR DREAMS MAY MEAN, THEREFORE, ULTIMATELY YOU ARE THE BEST EXPERT.

DREAMER AS THE SOURCE

It is widely believed that everything that happens in your dream is about you and not about anyone else. Once you take that on board, all your dream work starts to fall into place. No-one else can enter your inner world and interfere with your dreaming. Other people may be able to influence your thoughts and feelings, but never your dreams. They may cause you to have nightmares but the symbolism in those nightmares will all be of your own making. The key

BELOW RIGHT Dreams are a good way to monitor our emotional, mental and physical health.
BELOW Before you understand your dream you have to understand yourself, and what it is you might be trying to say to yourself.

to working with dreams is to understand what those symbols mean to you. What is it that your dreams are trying to tell you?

DREAMS AS A DIAGNOSTIC TOOL

The Greek philosopher, Aristotle, believed that dreams are a way of revealing to the dreamer what is physically wrong with the body, a sort of medical examination while you are asleep. In modern times we have been wary of paying much attention to his theory, but maybe there is something in it after all. Following in the footsteps of Freud and Jung, it is now fairly well established that dreams can be a diagnostic tool, used to determine the state of our psychological and spiritual health. When we are

A dream is the theatre in which the dreamer is himself the scene, the player, the prompter, the producer, the author, the public and the critic.

C G JUNG

THE RAT-INFESTED CAVERNS

A mother anxious about her daughter's health, experiences the following dream. It happened the night after the girl has gone for blood tests.

"That night I dreamed of boats in huge underground caverns. These boats were like barges and they were carrying vast cargoes all hidden and wrapped up in canvas, very bulky and awkward. They moved slowly and jerkily. There were thousands of them and the caverns were vast and, well, cavernous. I couldn't see what was lighting them but I had the impression of candles guttering in big candle-holders on the walls. I was standing on a sort of sidewalk which was running alive with rats.

It was obvious to me when I woke up that this was my way of trying to come to terms with my daughter's illness, which was a blood disease that had to be transported out of her system. The fact that I was an onlooker reflected my feeling of powerlessness, and the rats symbolized my secret horror of a situation I was trying hard to cope with."

going through a difficult time, such as a divorce or redundancy for instance, we would most likely expect our dreams to be disturbed, perhaps even nightmarish, containing hostile metaphors and imagery symbolic of anxiety and separation. Working with such dreams can be therapeutic, giving us an insight into what is happening at our core, beneath the veneer we present to the world.

AN EARLY WARNING SYSTEM

The unconscious mind is a storehouse of information. One way of accessing this information is through our dreams. When something is wrong for instance, our unconscious may try to bring it to our attention through a dream. In a sense, our dreams can give us a glimpse of the future; what is about to happen will first be symbolized in our dreams. The dream is like a whisper before the shouting begins. It is then up to us to heed that whisper and take action to avert the impending catastrophe.

Our dreams are like a good friend. They are always on our side and doing everything they can to help us. The only problem is that they speak a different language. To make the most of what they have to offer means learning that language.

WORKING WITH YOUR DREAMS

The unconscious is like a treasure chest, packed with revealing and important information that can help us on our journey through life. Our dreams are

a key to opening that chest, yet they are illusory and ephemeral, transient, fleeting and almost impossible to catch hold of. Dreams can't be wrestled into submission, but have to be seduced into giving up their secrets, teased into revealing their mysteries. A dream is to explore, to play with and to live with. It doesn't take too kindly to being dissected or analysed into submission. Dreams cannot be catalogued and filed away, graded and pigeonholed. They just don't operate like that. The same goes for recalling a dream. You can't demand that it be remembered. You have to sneak up on it, turn your back and wait as it shyly reveals itself. You need to half-close your eyes when you think of it and stop using your will to try and force it into the spotlight.

BELOW Our dreams are our early warning system that things are not as well as they might be; it is as well to pay heed, to listen. Our dreams are a part of us, not alien images beamed in from the outside.

DREAM RECALL

MANY PEOPLE CLAIM THAT THEY DO NOT DREAM. IT IS MUCH MORE LIKELY THAT THEY ARE UNABLE TO REMEMBER THEIR DREAMS. OUR DREAMS TEND TO SLIP AWAY, LIKE A THIEF IN THE NIGHT, BEFORE WE HAVE CHANCE TO APPREHEND THEM. YET OUR DREAMS ARE THE ONE PLACE WHERE WE CAN RELAX, WHERE WE CAN BE OURSELVES. OUR DREAMS ARE RIPPLES IN THE POOL OF OUR UNCONSCIOUS, THE PLACE WHERE THE WORRIES AND ANXIETIES THAT WE SO SUCCESSFULLY HIDE FROM THE WORLD MAY SURFACE IN SAFETY. DREAMS CAN GIVE US VALUABLE INSIGHTS INTO OUR LIVES, AND TO GET THE MOST OUT OF THEM, WE NEED TO TRAIN OURSELVES IN THE ART OF DREAM RECALL.

ABOVE Talking about dreams is a good way to defuse them, but also to begin to understand them. Women tend to talk about their dreams more than men, and express more of an interest in others' dreams.

DREAM JOURNALS

One of the best and easiest ways for remembering dreams is to keep a dream journal. It's worth keeping a special book or note pad and using it only for recording your dreams. Keep the book and a pen by your pillow and write in it as soon as you wake each morning. When you wake up, make as little physical movement as possible – even turning over can be enough for the memories to evaporate before you have had chance to record them. Lying still, in the same position as when you woke up, often increases dream recall. Keep your eyes closed. Not only will there be less distraction this way, but many people are often able to see the dream again.

If you can't remember any dreams, then just jot down feelings or thoughts that spring to mind. These may well be echoes of your last dream, a sort of dream vapour trail, and may be enough to trigger further memories of your dreams. If you wake up from a vivid dream in the middle of the night, it is a good idea to record it straightaway before going back to sleep. Some people keep a torch by the bed to save putting the bedside light on.

RECORDING DREAMS

There is no single, right way to record your dreams. You may want to jot down key words or feelings, or make a note of the people or events. Some people prefer to write a narrative of their dream while others like to include pictures or sketches. If you can't remember the start of your dream, don't give up. Don't worry about sequence; working backwards or from the middle can lead you to remember more details. Sometimes you'll be halfway through

RIGHT The more we keep a journal the more likely it is to actually influence our dreams – we begin to dream the journal. This makes analysing and understanding our dreams much easier.

remembering a dream when you'll remember something from dreams you had previously forgotten. Even fragments of dreams are valuable and can contain useful information. Writing in the present rather than the past tense can help you re-live the dream as you record it.

You might want to record your dream on one side of the page and leave the other side blank for comments and interpretation later on. It is, however, a good idea to record the date and the place where you had the dream and to generally include as much detail as possible; some people like to include the phase of the moon for instance. If you can't write the dream in your journal immediately you wake up, then make a note of the things you remember the most. These will jog your memory later on when you do have time to continue your journal.

THEMES AND PATTERNS

As you keep your journal, images, incidents and even emotions will slowly build over time to create a picture of your unique psychic identity, but you should keep the journal for at least a month before you try to make any sense of it. When you look, you may notice recurring themes or patterns in your

dreams. Perhaps a recurring vision of being chased, or falling from a high place, or being confined in a small place for instance. Or it might be a symbol, such as a flower, a road, a boat, or a particular animal that keeps cropping up. Recurring themes often indicate there is something in your life that needs your attention, perhaps a part of you that wants expression. You could also look for links between your dreams and events that happened recently. Identifying a pattern can make us better equipped to deal with life.

LEFT Dreaming of a particular symbol and seeing it crop up repeatedly might indicate an important theme that you need to work on.

ABOVE Recurring themes often indicate recurring worries. By paying attention to what the dream is trying to say to us we can help alleviate the stress.

A dream is an answer to a question we haven't yet learned how to ask. FOX MULDER, THE X-FILES

DREAM INVESTIGATION

HAVING LEARNED HOW TO RECALL AND RECORD YOUR DREAMS, THE NEXT STEP IS TO MAKE SOME SENSE OF THEM. BE WARY OF INSTANT INTERPRETATIONS OFFERED BY TRADITIONAL DREAM DICTIONARIES, HOWEVER USEFUL OR KNOWLEDGEABLE THEY MAY SEEM. OUR DREAMS ARE INFINITELY SUBTLE AND COMPLEX AND IT IS ALMOST IMPOSSIBLE TO ASCRIBE A CAST-IRON MEANING TO A SYMBOL. INSTEAD WE HAVE TO FIND CREATIVE WAYS OF WORKING WITH OUR DREAMS, PERHAPS USING INSIGHTS GAINED IN BOOKS OR FROM OTHERS TO HELP US, BUT ULTIMATELY DISCOVERING OUR OWN MEANING FROM DEEP WITHIN. THERE ARE MANY METHODS WE CAN ADAPT AND USE TO HELP US, SO WORK OUT THE BEST ONE FOR YOURSELF.

GESTALT TECHNIQUES

Fritz Perls was the 20th-century pioneer of Gestalt therapy. Perls said that dreams are "a message of yourself to yourself" and he saw everything in the dream as a representation of the dreamer's personal experience. The Gestalt method involves contacting different "parts" of yourself and exploring their meaning. For instance, in a recurring dream of being chased by a bear, you are both the bear and the one

BELOW RIGHT Once we wake we can calmly and quietly replay the dream and see what it means and where it comes from.
BELOW Keeping a dream journal will throw great light on the mysteries of our dreams.

being chased. You could then explore what it means for you to be the bear, considering for instance why he is chasing you. Maybe he is hungry and wants to eat you up, or perhaps he has an urgent message that he needs to give you, or it could be that he is someone else in disguise. There are many possible interpretations, but only you would know what the bear means in the context of your dream. To help you explore different aspects of yourself, it can be useful to sit in different chairs, or to use a different voice when you are "being" each of the characters. If you feel blocked and don't know what the "answer" is, make something up. You may be surprised to discover that it has some meaning. This "what part

of me and what is it saying?" approach to dreams seems to be particularly helpful for recurring dreams, or those dreams that are relatively short and uncomplicated, and which contain clear and easily recognisable symbolism.

FREE ASSOCIATION

In his therapeutic work, Freud used the technique of free association, encouraging his patient to let his or her thoughts "free wheel" from a starting point in the dream. This could be a word, feeling, object, person or symbol. To work with your dreams, take each element of the dream that you want to understand and write it down on a clean sheet of paper. Then, without thinking about it, write down whatever word comes to mind when you look at each element. Keep going until your chain of connections breaks down. You could use pictures or graphic symbols rather than words if you like.

DREAM DETECTIVE

Often the skill of dream interpretation lies in asking the right questions. You can try treating your dreams as clues to a mystery that you, the detective, are trying to solve. This means focusing particularly on those aspects of the dream that strike you as odd or disturbing in some way, and asking yourself a series of questions. For instance you could ask yourself how you feel about what is happening, if it reminds you of anything, or what your thoughts are. You may find that one question and answer leads naturally on to the next question and answer, and so on. It's rather like following a trail. When you reach a dead end with your questions, pick up on a different element of the dream and start again. You can also see if this dream detective technique works well with a partner. Someone else asking the questions can make the interpretation very different.

RIGHT Finding out what our dream is trying to say to us means we have to do some detective work – by exploring the symbolism that is unique to us we can access our subconscious desires and needs.

A dream that is not interpreted is like a letter that has not been opened. THE TALMUD

DREAM DETECTIVE

In the following dream, a young woman feels overwhelmed by emotion but can make no sense of what the dream may mean.

"I've never had a dream quite like it. I could see emotions in the air like great thick music notes. And every emotion was overwhelming. I was being played like some giant monstrous instrument. I was being plucked and strummed and fingered and drummed and thumped and blown and twanged all at once and every beat, every note was a new emotion. When I woke up I was drenched in sweat and feeling really sick, as if I had just been through the wringer. I felt limp for days unable to eat or think of anything else except this dream. It followed me round like a small insistent child that I couldn't ignore. I almost felt as if I wanted to pick it up and cuddle it, but I didn't know what it wanted."

Afterwards she played "dream detective" and asked herself a series of questions which proved quite revealing and seemed to open up the meaning of the dream.

Q: Are the emotions in the dream the same as I have been experiencing in my everyday life?

A: No, but they do seem familiar as if they are brooding just under the surface.

Q: Is there anything troubling me at the moment that is looking for emotional release?

A: I don't think so. I am quite happy at the moment, or at least I was until this dream. It has unsettled me and made me restless. Or was I restless anyway and this dream has made me focus on that?

Q: I wonder why I am restless?

A: I don't know. Since I got married six months ago I seem to have disappeared. I don't think my own thoughts anymore. I don't feel as if I exist. I am happy but I'm not thinking about things any more. Perhaps this dream is my way of getting in touch with myself, my emotions again?

PREPARE TO DREAM

PEOPLE HAVE ALWAYS SUSPECTED THAT THE INNER UNIVERSE OF OUR DREAMS IS A SOURCE OF WISDOM. THROUGHOUT HISTORY, DREAMS HAVE BEEN USED FOR HEALING, TO STIMULATE INVENTION AND DISCOVERY, AS WELL AS INSPIRE GREAT LITERATURE AND WORKS OF ART. THEY HAVE ALSO BEEN USED TO PREDICT THE FUTURE AND BRING SPIRITUAL REVELATION. FOR MOST OF US, MOST OF THE TIME, OUR DREAMS ARE NOT ON SUCH AN EPIC SCALE, BUT THEY ARE A VALUABLE SOURCE OF SELF-KNOWLEDGE. ONCE WE HAVE ACCEPTED THAT DREAMS ARE AN IMPORTANT PART OF OUR LIFE, WE WILL FIND THAT THEY BECOME MORE POTENT AND REVEALING. WE NEED, THEREFORE, TO FIND WAYS TO DREAM THE BEST POSSIBLE DREAMS.

A SHRINE FOR SLEEP

In the ancient world, dreams were "incubated" in sacred or lonely places, such as a temple or the wilderness, in order to create an ideal birth place for them. Take this principle into your own sleeping habits and transform your bedroom into a "shrine for sleep". Make sure the room is as comfortable and relaxing as possible. The temperature should be not too hot and not too cold, and there should be sufficient ventilation. Keep the space clear and free from clutter, and surround yourself with colours and objects that gently stimulate your senses in a positive way rather than depress you. Relaxing colours are lilacs, neutrals and pinks, although any shade that appeals to you is fine. Tidy away any objects that are associated with the outside world, such as shoes and clothes, and use soft lighting. Any kind of electrical equipment is best kept to a minimum in the bedroom.

BEDTIME RITUALS

In the past, societies who recognized the importance of dreaming created elaborate rituals to prepare body, mind and soul for the journey. To get the most from our dreams, we need to be in a relaxed, receptive state and approach going to sleep in a spirit of openness and enquiry. If we go to bed stressed or completely exhausted then we are unlikely to get the most from our dreams.

To get ourselves into the right frame of mind, we can create our own modern-day rituals to prepare for sleep and dreaming. One simple way of doing this is by listening to music. A little gentle classical music is a good choice, although you could experiment with other types of music to see if they have any effect on your sleep and dreaming patterns. Alternatively you could try burning incense or vaporizing essential oils in the evening. Useful scents include sandalwood as an aid to meditation and to

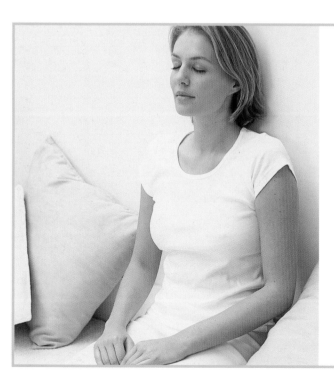

MEDITATION FOR DREAMS

When we meditate, we enter a state of altered consciousness. As body and mind unwind, our brain rhythms slow down to produce a relaxed alpha wave pattern, similar, yet of greater intensity, to that produced during deep sleep. In such a state, we become quiet and receptive. Try this meditation every night for a week and make a note in your dream journal of any changes to your sleep or dreams.

1 Sit in a relaxed position, close your eyes and focus on your breathing. As you breathe in, imagine a stream of golden light entering through the crown of your head.

2 Hold your breath for a few seconds, or as long as is comfortable and visualize the light circulating around your body.

3 Now breathe out, imagining the light leaving your body through the soles of your feet, taking away all the cares of the day.

4 Repeat the sequence several times.

You may want to experiment with breathing in different colours, depending on your changing needs. Pink is good for emotional healing, blue for calm, lavender for spiritual awareness, and green for fresh and original thinking.

ABOVE Creating a bedroom that is a shrine to sleep will help you to incubate dreams.
FAR LEFT Essential oils and scents can also help to create the right atmosphere for dreams and trouble-free sleep.
LEFT Bedroom rituals, such as taking a warm candlelit bath, are a good way to wind down for bed, free the mind from the day's troubles and make us more receptive to dreams.

connect with your higher self; lavender to encourage relaxation and calm; frankincense to open up to the angelic realm; and myrrh to connect with mysterious, archetypal energies. Experiment with other aromas, but make sure you choose scents that relax and soothe rather than ones that stimulate. A herb sachet placed under your pillow can also induce soothing sleep. Suitable fillers include dried hops, lavender, marjoram and passion flower.

Taking a warm, candlelit bath before bedtime is also a good way of letting go of the cares of the day in preparation for sleep. A couple of drops of essential oil can be swished into the water if you wish. Try practising a meditation technique last thing at night. It is a good way of switching off from your worldly concerns and creating a space for your unconscious to "come through" in the night without any worries and problems getting in the way.

Reach high, for stars lie hidden in your soul. Dream deep, for every dream precedes the goal.

PAMELA VAULL STARR

DREAM TOOLS

In many parts of the world, great store is set by dreams, for instance many African societies believe that dreams are linked to destiny. Dreams are seen as a vehicle for the spirit world to communicate with the dreamer, giving important information relating to health, enemies or the future. Among Native Americans there is a widespread belief that a "sacred power" speaks to you in your dreams. This power will often appear as an animal. In such societies dreams are taken seriously and dream tools are used to assist the dreamer in a variety of ways, especially for protection from bad dreams and to assist in dream programming and recall.

ABOVE We have access to a wide range of tools to help us interpret our dreams, including those used by other cultures.

DREAM WISDOM

People have always suspected that the inner universe of our dreams is a source of infinite wisdom. Throughout history, dreams have been used for healing, to stimulate invention and discovery, as well as inspiring great literature and works of art. They have also been used to predict the future and bring spiritual revelation. For most of us most of the time, our dreams do not fall into these epic categories, yet increasingly we are recognizing them as a valuable source of self-knowledge. Once we have accepted that dreams are an important part of our life, we will find that they become more potent and revealing. This means that we should prepare ourselves for the best possible dreams that we can have.

THE DREAM DOCTOR

The Cuna Indians of Central America see dreams as having an identity or power, with bad dreams signifying an impending disaster or illness. A disturbing dream would be taken to the "dream doctor" or medicine man for interpretation and a "prescription" to make it better.

Typically the prescription is an object into which special "power" or spells have been worked. The dream tool is then taken to bed by the dreamer to work its magic through the night and nullify the bad effects of the dream. Dream dolls and spearheads are the Cuna's most common dream tools, but stones, pegs, crosses and miniature weapons, such as axes or knives, are also used.

RIGHT A Cuna Native American woman, with a young girl beside her, takes care of a dream doll. As a potent dream tool the doll will be an integral part of the owner's daily life, linking the waking and dream worlds.

The dream doctor may also make up a powder containing a special wood mixed with black date palm and rub it over the dreamer's eyes to protect them from the effects of the bad dream. Through these actions it is believed that the dream's power is negated or "earthed".

SKY AXES

The Cuna Indians live on the islands off the Atlantic coast of Panama, and their lives are very much influenced by the weather and the natural elements. Violent storms during the night frequently disturb their sleep, and a favourite dream-doctor cure is to sleep with a "sky axe". Sky axes are real axe heads that have been found at the old burial ground sites of the Cuna people. The Cuna Indians believe that these axe heads help protect their dream spirit guides from the power of thunder by making the spirit guides invisible.

As we would expect, the dream tools used by the Cuna Indians and other indigenous peoples are intimately related to a specific culture and lifestyle. However, we can adapt the principle of dream tools to suit our particular circumstances and create our own tools to assist our dreaming.

YOUR OWN DREAM TOOLS

If you want to create your own dream tools, you need to choose objects that have special meaning for you. This could be an item that has special significance in your everyday life, or a childhood toy, a memento from a lover, a gift from a friend, or a treasured photo. If it is nature that inspires you, look for natural objects such as a piece of driftwood, a pebble from a favourite beach, a piece of tree bark or a fragrant flower. Dream tools can also be chosen to tie-in with the kind of dream you are trying to have or recall, maybe in answer to a particular question or on an important theme in your life. For instance, if work is an issue, then choose an object to symbolize what it is that you do: a tool for an engineer, a mixing spoon for a chef, a pen for a writer, or a thermometer for a nurse for instance.

ABOVE Like other Native American traditions, the Fox and Sauk tribe uses costume and ritual to help people recall and interpret their dreams.

EMPOWERING YOUR DREAM TOOL

Before a dream tool can work its magic, traditionally it is "empowered" by the dream doctor with special spells. You can do this yourself using colour and visualization. Use red for dreams of passion and adventure, blue or lilac for healing, green to be shown new pathways in life, and orange when looking at relationships. If you are working on communication issues, choose deep blue; for power and authority use purple; or work with yellow when seeking an answer to a health question. You could also use any other colours that intuitively spring to mind as being the ones that are most appropriate for you at the time.

To work with the colour, visualize your dream tool surrounded in coloured light, wrap the tool in a piece of the right coloured fabric or tie coloured ribbons on to the object. As you do so, spend some time visualizing the colour in your head, and mentally surround the item with it. When it is ready, take your dream object and put it under your pillow. It may help you have the sort of dream you want or else help protect you from bad dreams.

DREAM CATCHING

In Native American culture, dreams are seen as messages from sacred spirits in the night sky. Certain tribes also believe in the idea of the Great Dream. In the womb, everyone has their own great dream but this gets forgotten at birth. This dream bestows gifts

such as courage, creativity, humour or empathy upon the individual and gives a vision for the best pathway through life. From a young age, children are encouraged to "catch" and explore their dreams and young men will fast until they have a vision of their "song of life". Dream catching plays an important part in initiation ceremonies, where the initiate makes a magical or sacred circle around himself to "capture" the messages from the dream spirits in the space inside the circle. The dream catcher tool is a symbolic representation of this magical or sacred circle.

CATCH YOUR DREAMS

Dream catchers not only capture the good spirits, but also filter out any negative or unwanted powers. They consist of a cobweb-like structure on a circular frame, usually with beads or feathers attached to it. This structure symbolizes the "web of life"; in other words, it shows how all aspects of life are not separate but are intimately connected to one another. At the centre of the web sits Iktome, the spider, and keeper of dreams. Iktome is often represented by a coloured bead or shell. The dream catcher is hung near the sleeper's bed. The good dreams pass to Iktome, who holds them for the dreamer. The bad dreams are ensnared in her web and can be emptied away in the morning.

Dream catchers can be made in many shapes and sizes. They are not only useful but are also bright and colourful and make an interesting decoration in a bedroom. Children find them especially appealing and many parents have experienced positive results with children who suffer nightmares or who are afraid of the dark. Remember to empty the dream catcher each morning by tapping any unwanted dreams into the waste bin. Do this with the child, or encourage them to do it for him or herself.

MAKING A DREAM CATCHER

A good way of protecting yourself from disturbing dreams is to make your own dream catcher. It may also help you gain more insight into where you should be going in life and show you the best choices to help you achieve your ends. A dream catcher is a very personal thing and there is plenty of scope to make it in a way that appeals to you.

YOU WILL NEED

- a thin and bendy piece of wood about 60cm (2ft) long. A freshly cut piece of bamboo or hazel is ideal.
- a length of twine, such as fishing line or strong cotton thread
- feathers, a few beads and some coloured ribbons for decoration

1   Curl the bamboo or hazel into a circle and fasten it with twine wrapped around. Some people like to cover the whole of the wood in ribbon before they start, but it is up to you.
2   Cut off any sharp ends of wood at the join and wrap some ribbon around it.
3   Tie one end of the twine onto any point on the circle and tie it to the opposite point of the circle. Cut off the long end of twine.
4   Tie another piece of twine across the middle of the circle, at right angles to the first piece.
5   Attach four shorter pieces of twine between the four tying-on points to form a square. From the middle of one of the shorter lengths, attach a piece of twine to the two tying-on-points on the other side of the circle. Repeat for the other short lengths. This gives you a sort of "cat's cradle" effect. Experiment until you have a pleasing criss-cross of lines resembling a spider's web.
6   Add a bead in the centre to represent the spider.
7   Finish by decorating the dream catcher with some ribbons hanging from the bottom of the circle. Add some feathers and beads to these downward-hanging ribbons.

When your dream catcher is finished you can empower it in the same way as with a dream tool. Hang your dream catcher at the window of your bedroom, or above the bed.

ABOVE The dream catcher is a Native American device that filters your dreams so that only the pleasant ones get through.

DREAM GUIDES

Sometimes an ally or guide will appear in our dreams. In Native American culture, animals often symbolise these guides or helpers, with each person having their own totem or "power" animal. To find your totem animal, ask to be shown in a dream, or devise a dream journey to find it. This involves a visualization in which you see in your mind a path that you begin to walk down. As you walk, take notice of the scenery and the details around you, then open your mind and call for your power animal. The animal could be anything, from a wolf to a beetle, when it arrives greet it warmly, touch it and give it love. Be aware of what it feels like and feel the love it has for you. Remember, the greater the detail the more real it will be. Your dream guide might be an animal that you feel an affinity with in real life, you might love horses, for example, or feel inspired by the traditional north American wolf or bison, but don't try and manipulate the choice, let the animal make itself known to you.

CONTROLLING DREAMS

ALTHOUGH OUR DREAMS APPEAR TO BE OUT OF OUR CONTROL, WE CAN IN FACT TAKE A MORE ACTIVE ROLE AND LEARN HOW TO INFLUENCE OR PLAN THEM. THIS MAY NOT BE SOMETHING THAT YOU THINK IS POSSIBLE, BUT IF YOU ARE WILLING TO GIVE IT A TRY YOU MAY BE SURPRISED. WE CAN ASK OUR DREAMS TO PROVIDE US WITH ADVENTURES OR SELF-KNOWLEDGE OR SHOW US CREATIVE SOLUTIONS TO OUR PROBLEMS. WHEN WE ARE FEELING LOST WE CAN ASK OUR DREAMS FOR CLARITY AND GUIDANCE, INSPIRATION AND INFORMATION. WHAT WE ARE DOING IS ASKING FOR A MESSAGE FROM DEEP WITHIN OURSELVES, CONVEYED TO US BY WAY OF METAPHOR, MOOD AND SYMBOLS, VIA OUR DREAMS.

DEVELOPING DREAM SKILLS

Dreams speak in a language of pictures and feelings rather than thoughts and words. The greater our ability to sense and visualize, the more we are able to take control of our dreams. A good place to start is in everyday life. We can begin by really starting to notice the visual impact of the world around us, observing the colours, shapes and textures more profoundly. Spend some time soaking up visual imagery that you find interesting. For instance this could include looking at paintings and works of art, tarot cards, mandalas or any other pictures that appeal to your senses. At the same time, pay more attention to your feeling state. Be aware of those things that alter your mood, noticing not only what you see, but also what you hear and maybe smell. Listening to music and reading is another way of developing your imagination and sensitivity.

CLEAR INTENTION

In the first instance, to plan a dream means having a good idea of why you want it and what it is exactly that you expect from it. The more sincere you are, the more likely is the chance that your unconscious mind will co-operate with you. Perhaps you need to work out some aspect of a relationship, or maybe you are trying to make an important decision and are not quite sure which way to go. Drawing on information from our dreams can give us a very clear idea of where we really want to be rather than where we think we ought to be.

SETTING THE SCENE

If you want to generate a particular type of dream, first you need to be in a relaxed and open frame of mind. Next you need to focus on what it is you want to dream about. This could mean writing it out

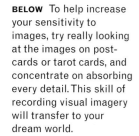

BELOW To help increase your sensitivity to images, try really looking at the images on post-cards or tarot cards, and concentrate on absorbing every detail. This skill of recording visual imagery will transfer to your dream world.

Don't be afraid of the space between your dreams and reality. If you can dream it, you can make it so.

LIFE DIRECTION

A young man is unsure about his direction in life so he asks for guidance in his dream.

"I really wanted to know where I was going, what I was supposed to be doing. I played some soothing music as I went to bed and let my mind go blank. I was asking for guidance as I fell asleep. I had an amazing dream in which I was riding a camel across the desert. All I really remember was the utter silence, the loneliness and isolation, but also a real feeling of peacefulness.

The message of the dream seemed very clear to me. 'Go alone and with nothing until you are ready to be with people again.' It all made perfect sense to me, and helped me a great deal."

LEFT Dreaming Bread – an old recipe for making your dreams come true. Perhaps an old wives' tale, but perhaps also a method of triggering a dream event, the act of performing any kind of ritual has its own potency.

on a piece of paper and tucking it under your pillow. You could also write in your dream journal. If you have any questions, make sure they are as open-ended as possible. Repeat your requests to yourself just before going to sleep. Sometimes holding an object that is connected with the situation is helpful. Reviewing the events of the day last thing at night may also help you relate your dream to what is happening in everyday life. A good way of training your mind in this way is to add an element of ritual to your bedtime routine.

DREAMING BREAD

You might like to try this traditional ritual for generating dreams. It involves making a "dreaming bread". You can use an ordinary bread recipe but bake a round loaf. As you knead the dough concentrate on what sort of dream you want to have. When baked cut the bread into three and take a bite out of each piece. Put the remaining pieces under your pillow and that night it is said that you will dream your requested dream, as long as you don't speak between eating the bread and sleeping.

BELOW LEFT Listening to music can also help you to develop your imagination and sensitivity. But make sure you really listen, use your mind to process the sounds rather than just letting it wash over you.
BELOW By creating the right atmosphere, and performing simple rituals, our dream work can become more connected.

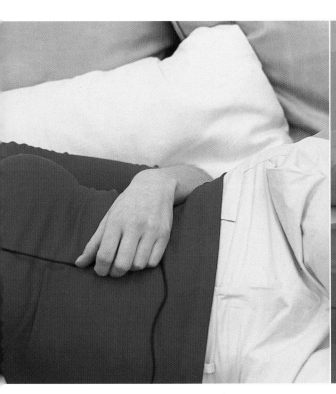

PROBLEMS AND INSPIRATION

THERE IS A TENDENCY TO SEE PROBLEMS AS A SERIES OF HAZARDS TO BE AVOIDED, OR ELSE HINDRANCES TO BE SKILFULLY NEGOTIATED. WHEN WE HAVE A PROBLEM, MOST OF US WANT TO SOLVE IT AS QUICKLY AS POSSIBLE. HOWEVER, IT IS ALSO POSSIBLE TO SEE PROBLEMS AS CHALLENGES. PROBLEMS PRESENT AN OPPORTUNITY TO LEARN AND GROW, TO CHANGE AND IMPROVE. SOMETIMES A PROBLEM IS A GATEWAY TO A BETTER FUTURE. IF WE RUSH AT SOLVING OUR PROBLEMS INSTEAD OF TRYING TO LEARN FROM THEM WE RISK NOT GROWING, NOT LEARNING. WE CAN ALSO USE OUR DREAMS TO HELP US. IF WE ARE PERCEPTIVE ENOUGH THE SOLUTION MAY BE SOMETHING WE WOULD NEVER HAVE THOUGHT OF.

SLEEP ON IT

Some of the most creative solutions to problems have not come through logic or reasoning but through dreams. For instance, in the 19th century, Dmitri Mendeleyev, a Russian chemist, was having a problem about how to organize chemical elements. Deciding to "sleep on it" he had a dream in which he saw the elements falling in the correct order. Using the information from his dream, he went on to devise the periodic table of elements, a central concept of modern inorganic chemistry.

Creative solutions do not arrive out of the blue however. They are usually preceded by plenty of "spade work", which may have taken days, weeks, months or even years before the final flash of genius. A shift in perception seems to happen more easily when the logical mind has given up on the problem. When we relax and stop trying, our innate, inner intelligence can take over and put the pieces of the puzzle together while we sleep.

DECODING THE MESSAGE

It can sometimes be the smallest detail in a dream that can provide the clue to help us solve the problem or dilemma we are working on. It might be a visual image or symbol, a smell or a sound, a mood or a feeling. It is a question of being alert and allowing intuition, rather than the conscious mind, to help us solve the riddle.

While we sleep, the mind continues to work. Freed from the restraints of logic and convention, the unconscious is free to take an unorthodox

LEFT Our dreams can expose what lies beneath the surface, thoughts or emotions that were hidden. In the same way they can help with problem solving, bringing a solution up to the surface of our consciousness.

All this inventing, this producing, takes place in a pleasing lively dream.   WOLFGANG AMADEUS MOZART

WORKING WITH DREAMS

86

RIGHT Our mind doesn't go to sleep when our body does; it begins its most creative work. When we are awake it is to our benefit to try and decode that work, to access the creative part of ourselves.

approach to the problem and come up with a solution. It is not even necessary to be able to remember our dreams for this process to work. Most of us will have experienced being unable to solve a problem one day, but the next, after a good night's sleep, suddenly finding that either a new way of looking at the problem has appeared, or the problem itself has vanished. If you enjoy completing crossword puzzles, you could test this theory on a superficial level. Find a clue that you're unable to crack, and just before you go to sleep run it through your mind. The next day, revisit the clue and see if the answer comes to you.

DREAMS TO INSPIRE

Many writers, artists and musicians have literally "dreamed up" stories, poems, melodies and other works of art. For instance, Robert Louis Stevenson, the 19th-century Scottish writer, spent days wracking his brains for a suitable plot to explore the idea that we all have our good and bad sides. He claimed that the storyline for his novel *The Strange Case of Dr Jekyll and Mr Hyde* came to him in a dream. More recently, the famous surrealist paintings of 20th-century artists such as Salvador Dalí or René Magritte are set in dream-like landscapes, while singer-songwriter Paul McCartney says the Beatles' hit-song "Yesterday" was in his head when he woke up one morning.

BELOW Dreams have always inspired writers and artists and painters – they can still inspire us, motivate us, stimulate and encourage us. Will your dreams help to complete the jigsaw of your waking life?

DREAM DECISION

A young man is having trouble making a decision about a job offer. After a day thinking out the pros and cons, he decides to sleep on the problem, and before he falls asleep deliberately places in his mind the problem that is preoccupying him.

"I couldn't work out whether I should take the job I was being offered. On paper it seemed to be just what I was looking for, but something was holding me back. I couldn't make a decision. I went to sleep wondering about this and had a dream where I saw myself smoking a cigar. That was all. I couldn't remember anything else but the dream struck me as very evocative, very symbolic.

The cigar seemed to represent everything that was holding me back about taking that job. It represented success, winning and achievement and being like my father. I could almost smell myself in a city suit, all aftershave and cigar smoke, like a banker or a tycoon. It wasn't an image I liked and I realized it wasn't a job I really wanted, so I turned it down. The cigar made me realize that I was thinking about taking the job because it was what my father would have wanted, but it wasn't me."

DREAMS AND RELATIONSHIPS

WE ARE SOCIAL BEINGS AND OUR INTERACTIONS WITH ONE ANOTHER AFFECT US DEEPLY. RELATIONSHIPS OF ONE KIND OR ANOTHER WEAVE THE FABRIC OF LIFE, FORMING A RICH TAPESTRY. SOME OF THESE RELATIONSHIPS ARE RELATIVELY SUPERFICIAL, WHILE OTHERS HAVE THE POWER TO AFFECT US AT A DEEP EMOTIONAL LEVEL – FOR GOOD OR BAD. OUR DREAMS CAN GIVE US GREAT INSIGHT INTO OUR RELATIONSHIPS WITH LOVERS, FRIENDS, FAMILY OR COLLEAGUES. THEY CAN HIGHLIGHT AREAS OF TENSION, REVEAL THINGS, ANSWER OUR QUESTIONS AND HELP US COME TO TERMS WITH OUR FEELINGS. WE CAN USE OUR DREAMS AS A "WAY IN" TO HELPING IMPROVE THE RELATIONSHIPS THAT MATTER TO US MOST.

ABOVE Dreams about relationships can act as a way in to understanding them more. Don't dismiss even the most banal ones, as they still could be a way of accessing how you really feel about people close to you.

MAKING SENSE OF IT ALL

Sometimes it is tricky to disentangle the messages carried in a dream. Another person appearing in a dream may be representing an aspect of the dreamer's own psyche rather than themselves. Other people may also appear in disguise as an animal or an inanimate object for instance. We also have to remember that our dreams are not our everyday lives being acted out. They are an attempt by the unconscious to comment on and try and make some sense of what is going on for us. They can reveal what is frightening or worrying us, what is making us happy or sad, jealous or angry, and what we need to further growth and development.

When using your dreams to work on relationships, avoid the temptation to come up with a quick and easy interpretation. You need to tread

carefully and keep asking yourself "have I got this right?" It may also be helpful for close friends or partners to work on their dreams together, checking the meaning of the dream with one another. This can be an exciting journey of discovery and strengthen the bond that is between you.

Of course it isn't just our lover that we might dream about. All sorts of other relationships are reflected in our dreaming – children, friends, colleagues, even enemies or mere acquaintances. How we view our relationships in our dreams can indicate how we really view them on a waking level – without the need for any social niceties. We may find that the relationships no longer sustain or support us, or that they need some care and attention. What our dreams can tell us is dependent on how honest we are with ourselves.

Personal relations are the important thing for ever and ever.   E M FORSTER

DREAM DETECTION

A good place to start doing some relationship work is to play "dream detective" and begin by asking some basic questions about the dream. By working through them, you will gain a lot of insight into what the dream is trying to tell you, which is very different from interpretation. The questions can be used to investigate any type of relationship that you wish to explore, not only sexual partnerships.

DREAM QUESTIONNAIRE

Asking the following questions may help to unlock the symbolism of your relationship dreams.

1 What exactly are you doing in the dream? How are you doing it? Describe your thoughts and feelings as you do it.

2 What aren't you doing in the dream? Is there anything specifically missing from the dream that is important, anything that you feel you should or want to be doing?

3 Imagine the dream is a play being acted out and you can rewrite any section of it. Which bits would you re-script and why? With regard to what you are doing, how would you replay the action of the dream differently?

4 Is there anything in the dream that remains unfinished or that you would like to know more about? Is there anything in the dream that brings up conflicts that you feel have not been dealt with in the dream?

5 How do your actions (and those of anyone else in the dream) parallel your actions in daily life? How far are they similar and how far are they different? If they are different, can you think of any reasons why this might be so?

6 If this dream were a film or play, what sort of film or play would it suggest to you? For instance, would it be a romance, a thriller, a comedy, a farce or an adventure story? How does this correspond with daily life? How is it different?

7 If this dream were an educational device for relationship training, what message would it be teaching? What are you learning from the dream? Does it provide any useful insights into the relationship?

8 How will you apply these insights from the dream to your everyday life? What will you do with the information you have gained from the dream?

ABOVE The relationships we have with peers are often some of the most formative and influential of our lives.
LEFT Once we become parents our emotional lives take on a whole new depth. This could well be reflected in our dreams.
BELOW Close friendships can be sustaining and supportive, but can also create angst and turmoil in our lives. Examine your dreams for clues to how you really feel about those who are closest to you.

ABOVE Acting out a dream might be impossible, and certainly impracticable. But if there is a possibility of at least recreating some part or proportion of a significant dream you are exploring, then why not try it?

WORKING WITH THE RELATIONSHIP QUESTIONNAIRE

To understand how the relationship questionnaire might be used, we can use the example of a dream had by a young man named Billy. In the dream, Billy and his girlfriend are at a railway station standing on opposite sides of the track when an express train whooshes into the station. The train doesn't stop, but when it leaves, Billy's girlfriend has disappeared.

A classic Freudian interpretation of the dream would be that the express train is a phallic symbol. It represents Billy's fear of losing his sexual prowess and the sadness he feels when his girlfriend leaves him as a result. However when Billy worked through the dream relationship questionnaire, he arrived at very different conclusions, none of which related to his sexuality. He saw the dream as a message that life was passing him by and he needed to take more risks rather than being a bystander.

WORKING WITH THE DREAM

This is how Billy works through the dream that he feels is about his relationship with his girlfriend.

"My girlfriend and I are standing on opposite sides of the railway tracks at the station. We are waving to each other. An express train comes between us and when it is going she has disappeared. I remember feeling very sad and wondering how she had got on the express train when it hadn't stopped."

Billy's answers and insights

1   I am waving at my girlfriend and I feel sad when she disappears. I am thinking about the mechanics of her disappearance as if it is a magic show at a theatre.

2   I am not going anywhere. I realize the reason I came to the station was to see her off. She was going away somewhere, not me. I am staying.

3   If I could rewrite the dream I wouldn't change anything except I wouldn't feel sad about her leaving. Now I realize that the sadness isn't about her going away but is about me not understanding how the trick was done.

4   The dream didn't bring up any conflict but it did make me realize that my girlfriend going away wasn't such a bad idea. In fact I feel our relationship isn't going anywhere but I have no idea what to do about it.

5   I think my actions in the dream are pretty similar to those in real life. I didn't behave any differently in the dream.

6   I think this would be a spy story, some sort of mystery or thriller. I guess I would like my life to be a bit more exciting and I think I'm actually a bit bored with my relationship.

7   To me the message is loud and clear. The dream teaches me that this relationship isn't going anywhere and I really ought to do something about it. It also makes me realize that it isn't just the relationship that is wrong, but my whole life is somehow over-ripe. I'm getting lazy and stuck in my ways. Deep down I think I'd like to go travelling or take up a dangerous sport or do something to wake myself up a bit.

8   The dream is trying to tell me that I have to take some action. I need to get off my backside and achieve more instead of watching other people have all the fun. I need to take some risks, make my life more exciting and enjoy being alive more.

FREE ASSOCIATION TECHNIQUE

You can take any element from a dream and use it as a starting point for free association. This means you can work with feelings as well as objects, people or places. Billy also used this technique with his express train dream, starting from the word "train". Interestingly, he arrived at a similar understanding as when he completed the dream relationship questionnaire: that he needed to take more control of his life.

TRIGGERING DREAM RECALL

Sometimes the more we look for meaning in our dreams the more such a meaning seems to elude us, or slip away. We can use techniques used in business to improve creativity and see if they might not also work with dream interpretation. For instance opening a book at random and seeing if any words that catch our eye there might trigger a memory or meaning. You could also try combining odd sequences in the dream and trying to tell a story using them. Or how about sleeping on it – using the next dream to see if it will make sense of the dream we are worrying about. It doesn't have to be a full night's sleep; try just having a quick nap and nod off thinking about your dream.

ACTING IT OUT

If you are feeling adventurous, you could try acting your dream out. This could literally mean going to a place that resembles your dream location and imagining yourself back in the dream. Alternatively, you could act it out at home, setting up a "stage" with the relevant props and characters. This exercise can be very effective when you do it with someone else. It may not always be appropriate to act out relationship dreams with the person you are dreaming about. Sometimes someone who is neutral in the relationship makes a better sounding board.

ABOVE Working with your dreams can take place at any time and in any place, all you need are a few quiet moments when you can focus your mind on your dream. Relax and allow your mind to drift.

BELOW LEFT Sitting quietly in a meditative state can often help us unlock the key to a dream's meaning.
BELOW Sometimes we need to turn our attention elsewhere and stop thinking about a dream. Try to do something completely different, and see if it rises to the surface of your mind.

BELOW RIGHT Our dreaming isolates us and makes us aware of the fragile and vulnerable parts of ourselves. This is nature's way of making us turn inwards and begin to question what our dreams mean.

BELOW While we sleep, doorways open in our mind, and our dreaming self takes wings and becomes capable of anything. In the world of dreams the impossible becomes achievable.

USING GESTALT

A good way of understanding our dreams is to assume that everything in the dream is an aspect of ourselves. Gestalt techniques are based on this principle. Applying them to his dream, first Billy "became" the train. He discovered that this part of him moves very fast, is forging full steam ahead and has no time to stop for anything or anyone. Next he was the rail track. He thought that this showed him that the fast part of him is "on track", moving ahead to a goal. To be on this track means leaving behind a part of himself, the onlooker who is waving "goodbye". The tracks are also what keep him separate from his girlfriend. When he thought about the dream some more, he realized that his girlfriend represented the part of himself that wants to move forwards, that wants to jump on the train and go off and have adventures, but there is another part holding him back, keeping him at the station. This brought him to the wave goodbye. At first when he had the dream, he thought the wave meant he was saying "goodbye" to his girlfriend and was feeling sad because of the separation from her. Now he wondered if the sadness was because he was separated from that vital, exciting part of himself that is prepared to jump on moving trains while he stays stuck at the station. It was like waving goodbye to his freedom and sense of adventure.

OPPOSITES

Another interesting way of working on relationship issues is to turn the Gestalt technique on its head and assume everything in the dream is the other person. In Billy's dream for instance, his girlfriend becomes the train. Looking at it like this, Billy thought it meant that she is moving too fast for him, and needed a more committed relationship than he felt he was ready for. Thinking about her as the station, he saw that she represented a stopping off point in his life. She is not the partner with whom he wants to journey through life with.

HIDDEN MESSAGES IN DREAMS

Sometimes it is not so obvious that a dream is about a relationship. However, we can rest assured that whenever we have a relationship issue, it will surface

in our dreams in one guise or another. We can assume that the dream is about the problem that is worrying us, and we can try to understand it in this light. This happened to a young woman called Sandra. She was worried that her partner didn't care for her, despite the fact that he told her he loved her. She thought he wanted to leave the relationship. She then had a mysterious dream about a sailing boat with a red sail going round in circles on a lake. The person sailing the boat was a stranger, not her boyfriend. In the dream she felt worried the boat was going to capsize and there would be no one to rescue the sailor.

Using the Gestalt technique with her dream, Sandra concluded that her sense of impending disaster had nothing to do with her boyfriend but was being generated from within herself. The boat represented the relationship, and she and not her boyfriend was the one who was "rocking" it. It was as though a part of her wanted to sabotage the relationship, the part that feels claustrophobic and uneasy. She realized that in some ways she felt trapped in the relationship, that it was not going anywhere, but "round in circles". The red sail spelled danger to her, a signal to look where she was going and keep out of dangerous waters.

ABOVE In our dreams we may be faced with decisions that need to be made, choices that are reflected in our waking life. These choices may be represented by doorways or paths. Your dream is reminding you to act, not avoid.

USING MYTHS AND LEGENDS

If you enjoy and are familiar with myths and legends, you could also use these to gain insight into your relationship dreams. For instance, you could use the Arthurian legends as archetypes for dream understanding. They are a rich picking ground for all sorts of relationships, ranging from the fairly commonplace to the bizarre. You could imagine yourself in the same situation as one of the characters and notice how the story turns out. Alternatively you could consider what "message" the legend has for you.

In the Arthurian legends there are many archetypes and relationship situations that you can work with. The main characters are as follows: Arthur, a king who stands for many different aspects of the Great Father, is married to Guinevere. She meanwhile is in love with Lancelot, Arthur's closest friend. Their affair causes Lancelot to betray Arthur. Morgan le Fay, Arthur's half-sister and a powerful sorceress, has a supposedly incestuous relationship with him. Merlin, the archetypal wise old man is obsessed with a young girl, while the archetypal hero, Sir Galahad, is celibate and devoted to purity.

ACKNOWLEDGEMENTS

Unless specified images used in the book belong to Anness Publishing Ltd. With thanks to the following agencies for additional images:

Art Archive: 10–11 *The Dream of Aescupalius*, Accademia Venice/Dagli Orti; 12t Musée du Louvre/Dagli Orti; 13t Eileen Tweedy, 14l Egyptian Museum/Dagli Orti; 14r *Ruins of Thebes* by Carl Richard Lepsius, Musée du Louvre/Dagli Orti; 17t National Archaeological Museum, Athens/Dagli Orti; 19 *The Death of Julius Caesar* by Vincenzo Camuccini, Galleria d'Arte Moderna, Rome/Dagli Orti; 20 V&A Museum, London/Eileen Tweedy; 23 British Library; 26 *The Dream of Tartini*, National Museum Budapest/Dagli Orti; 27b Bibliothéque Municipale Poitiers/Dagli Orti; 32r Turkish and Islamic Art Museum, Istanbul/Harper Collins Publishers; 33t *Joseph explaining the dreams of Pharoah* by Jean Adrien Guignet, Musée des Beaux Arts, Rouen/Dagli Orti; 44 Ocean Memorabilia Collection; 55tr *The Guest of Stone* by Marco Marcola, Museo Civico Sartorio Trieste/Dagli Orti; 66 *Dulle Griet*, detail, by Pieter Breughel the Elder, Mayer van den Bergh Museum; 70–1 *Ossian's Lament* by Karoly Kisfaludy, National Gallery, Budapest/Dagli Orti.

Corbis: 9t Dianna Sarto; 9b Sygma; 12b Gianni Dagli Orti; 15r Marc Garanger; 16 *Calliope and Homer* by Antonio Canova, Archivo Iconografico, SA; 17b Ruggero Vanni; 18l Raphael, School of Athens, detail, Ted Spiegel; 18r Araldo de Luca; 22tl Richard A. Cooke; 22tr Dallas & John Heaton; 22b Craig Lovell; 24br Elio Ciol; 25t Greenhalf Photography; 25b Richard Hamilton Smith; 27t *The Witch* by David Ryckaert III, Ali Meyer; 28 Penny Tweedie; 29tl Ralph A. Clevenger; 29tr Otto Rogge; 30tl Tom Bean; 30tr Dave Bartruff; 30b Bob Rowan/Progressive Image; 31 Geoffrey Clements; 32l Chris Lisle; 33b *The Annunciation* by Edward Burne Jones, Christie's Images; 34–5 David Pu'u; 36 Charles Gupton; 37t Ron Lowery; 37bl Ryszard Horowitz; 37br Richard Cummins; 38 Sigmund Freud by Bettmann; 39t John Lund; 39bl Larry Williams; 40bl Carl Jung by Bettmann; 41tl Rick Gayle; 41tr Ron Lowery; 42l Benjamin Rondel; 42r David Pu'u; 43 Mark Cooper; 45t, 45b James Nazz; 46 Chris Lisle; 47l William Whitehurst; 47r David Aubrey; 48r Dale O'Dell; 49t Chris Hellier; 49br Chris Rainer; 50l Phil Banko; 50r Firefly Productions; 51 Shutter & Mouse; 52–3 *Destruction of Jerusalem* by Ercole de'Roberti, Historical Picture Archive; 55tl Stapleton Collection; 55b Roy McMahon; 56r Todd A. Gipstein; 58 *O Holy night* by Henry Raymond, Christie's Images; 59r *Maiden and Unicorn*, Araldo de Luca; 60 Art Becker Photo; 61t Ron Lowery; 62l Jim Zuckerman; 62r Jose Luis Peleaz, Inc.; 63t Douglas Kirkland; 65br Dale O'Dell; 68 Richard T. Nowitz; 69l Ron Lowery; 69r Norbert Schaefer; 72l George Shelley; 72r Denis Scott; 73 Dale O'Dell; 76l LWA-JDC; 77 Pete Saloutos; 79t Denis Anthony Valentine; 80 Ron Watts; 81t Danny Lehman; 81c Lindsay Hebberd; 86 Denis Scott; 87b Mendola/Jeff Mangiat; 90 Thomas Schweizer; 91t LWA/Stephen Welstead; 92r Mauro PancLowery.

INDEX